LIVING WELL PAST 60

Also by George H. Hess, M. D.

Living At Your Best
With Multiple Sclerosis

Living Well
Past 60

George H. Hess, M.D.

Life Sciences Press
Tacoma, WA

Disclaimer

While it may be your constitutional right to implement the methods described in this book, it is suggested that you not undertake any diet, nutritional regimen or program or exercise without the direct supervision of a licensed and fully qualified practitioner.

Copyright © 1993 by George H. Hess

All rights reserved. Printed in U.S.A.

Library of Congress Cataloging - CIP
93-079233

ISBN 0-943685-17-6

Life Science Press, P.O. Box 1174, Tacoma, WA 98401

First printing, July, 1993

Cover photograph by Peggy Stevens.

DEDICATION

To Adriana: her companionship transformed my retirement into an adventure.

ACKNOWLEDGMENTS

No one is an island. Each of us is indebted to others for some part of every success we may achieve. In my case, I am the product of genes from American ancestors that were shaped by growing up in a Chicago, three generational household. Home, church and schools contributed to my education and world view. The University of Wisconsin gave me my Bachelor of Arts and Doctor of Medicine degrees. Living in a community and sharing the problems of my patients continued my education. Then at retirement came other opportunities.

The Tacoma and Pierce County Council on Aging, its directors and editors, encouraged and assisted my initial publications in Senior Scene. There would not have been a book without this stimulating interest in medical matters as they relate to older persons.

Specific help in producing this book must be credited to John Ullis and his knowledgeable staff at Quantum Computers. Transcribing newsprint to computer disc and rearrangement of articles was simplified through the genius of Apple hard and soft ware. Geriatrician Bruce Bannister, D.O. from the Department of Family Practice, University of Nevada School of Medicine, read the rough manuscript to suggest corrections and changes for updating the text.

CONTENTS

INTRODUCTION

I once asked a civic leader where he got all his good ideas. He replied that he liked to sit in the park and talk to the "old bums" he found there. Oldsters had both the experience and the time to sit around and think critically about the world's problems, he said.

After I retired from the general practice of medicine to become an "old bum," I, too, had the time and maturity to go critical. One of whom I was critical was the Rev. Harold (Hal) Reinhardt, Director of the Tacoma-Pierce County Council on Aging. Hal sent out a monthly newsletter called, *The Senior Scene* . A regular column in the paper was called, "To your good health," which offered nutritional advice to the retired elderly.

Hal had read a Lutheran Mission report from some Third World country which stated that the main source of vitamin C and iron for children was powdered milk sent from the United States. So his article advised seniors in need of vitamin C and iron to drink milk. When I pointed out that vitamins and minerals were only added to milk for export and not present in local dry milk, Hal suggested that I write the column.

So I began writing *Doctor's RX** and did so every month for nine years. But eventually I had to stop because the IRS made writing much too ex-

*RX is the medical symbol found on prescriptions. Back when doctors wrote prescriptions in Latin to pharmacist, it was a comand. Recepare means "you take," and then follow the ingredient list and direction, much as one would a cake recipe.

pensive for me to want to continue. The IRS considered my writing a form of "personal amusement" and would not allow me to claim as business expenses the university courses I took to stay current with the ongoing changes in medicine, as well as my annual license fees.

Writing is work, but it is kind of fun too. First, there is the research involved, and then the matter of putting together words, phrases and ideas to convey something meaningful and of value to others. Relatives and others have often turned to me for free medical advice. The topics I've chosen to write about here are simply little essays about the health problems encountered by the retired and the elderly.

I have enjoyed remembering and recounting some of my personal experiences in the following pages. Every senior should try autobiographical writing.

Over the years, some common but universal problems merited a repeat essay with a new approach. These have been edited and combined under a single subject. In like manner, I've incorporated many new scientific revelations concerning age which were unknown at the time of my original columns.

Oftentimes, as I have found, patients need explanations. They will act intelligently if they know how the body works, what causes illness, how to prevent it, and how remedies are supposed to work.

Busy doctors don't volunteer such information and few patients ask questions. But please be aware that I write of specific subjects only in very general terms. This is not a medical textbook, but it will impart a greater understanding and appreciation of medical terms and subjects. When you require treatment or in-depth advice, turn to your doctor, not this book.

The Nation's Health, a 1990 study published by the American Health Association, points out that the longer living elderly have been "rescued" from death. The "new survivors" now are more susceptible to chronic debilitating diseases. Twenty-five percent of this group live below the poverty level, and 30 percent live in substandard housing.

Women live seven years longer than men and many women were married to men older than themselves. Now 20 percent of women are widows at 60. By age 65 half have lost their husbands. Two thirds of women are alone at age 75. While African Americans make up 11 percent of the population, they constitute only 7.8 percent of those over the age of 65. Most Spanish Americans, with a life expectancy of 57 years, and Native Americans, with a life expectancy only 44 years, don't live long enough to collect benefits from Social Security and Medicare. Poverty is the norm for most elderly in this wealthiest of nations.

Hospitalization to solve our social problems is inappropriate. The elderly who are institutionalized decline quickly because neglect is their usual treatment. By achieving a ripe age, the elderly have shown great strength to endure, but past 60, they are subjected to more stresses than any other age group. Many must learn to cope with chronic conditions for which there is no cure. Age diminishes recuperative powers, so it is very important that the elderly prevent illnesses and injury. For these and other reasons, seniors have an obligation to take care of themselves. This book was written to help you enjoy retirement by preserving your health. I trust you will find the reading pleasurable as well.

1

UNDERSTANDING AGE

Aging

> *"I've known a great many people who lived into their 80s and 90s despite bad hearts, emphysema, arthritis, and other diseases. But the one thing all these people had in common was that they were creative. They had things they wanted to do; they had no reason to die. They had an appointment with life instead of with death. There was always comething that had to be accomplished and so the aging process was deferred just as death was deferred."*
>
> — Norman Cousins

How time flies! It seems only yesterday that I was a boy playing in Chicago's Midway Park. I like to remember a massive, larger-than-life sculpture at one end of the park. The sculpture was called "Time." It was a cowled figure, and contrary to how we are accustomed to think about time, it appeared to be very still rather than flying. The figure watched over a sea of humanity as it flowed by. This human sea begins as a crowded pool of infants and frolicking children which quickly ripples into churning waves of adults. The big people busy themselves doing the work of the world. Then this surge of humanity reaches a crest and breaks across a flat and calmer sea. Here there are fewer people and they appear elderly. Some look back at the crest. Others, halt and lame, seem only to strive for the nearby heavenly shore.

Does time pass? Memory brings past events into the present. The interval between "then" and "now" becomes timeless. Thus, time, in a metaphysical sense, can fly away and disappear, as it often does. Yet we remain aware of that interval in our lives. We realize that our activities in the past largely determine where we are, who we are and what we are today. This is particularly true of our present health. The "slings and arrows of outrageous fortune" do leave their mark. As a patient once put it, "If I'd known I was going to live so long, I'd have taken better care of myself."

We change as we age. Physical strength and agility diminish. Few of us participate in active sports after 40. In youth our kidneys and livers have capacities that far exceed demand. By the time we are ready to retire, these organs have lost half of their ability to detoxify and excrete toxins.

Our pulmonary connective tissue loses elasticity so that some emphysema is present in the lungs of all seniors. Smoking accelerates this normal aging of lungs. Emphysema can cripple an individual at a time of life when one might otherwise still be active. Kicking the smoking habit now is not too late. It will assist the labored breathing and alleviate the strangling cough.

Mice live 10 to 20 percent longer when they are not caged, but free to run and exercise. If you would "enjoy the best years for which the first were made," keep physically active. Involve yourself more with your family and community. Many of the degenerative diseases that come in the "golf-cart" age will respond to exercise. Vigorous added years are to be preferred over a destiny of medicated survival.

There is an unprecedented "graying" of America. In the last 30 years America's senior population has grown twice as fast as the general population. This is partly due to a declining birth rate. But in this century, sanitation, immunization and therapy for certain diseases have made long life a reality for all who follow healthy practices. Poverty, poor nutrition and injurious lifestyles are today the main factors undermining the health of most Americans.

Life expectancy at the time Rome ruled the world was only 25 years. Maximum life span then, as now, is around 115. At present, average longevity is more than 72 years. The increase in average life expectancy, however, is not accompanied by an increase in the health of older people. The rate of sickness and disability among the elderly is about the same as 50 years ago. Medical advances have been made chiefly in the area of childhood diseases. More young people survive today, pushing up average life expectancy. Chronic diseases associated with aging —cancer, arteriosclerosis, arthritis, diabetes, liver and kidney ailments — remain largely refractory to treatment. And while more people are living longer, they are not necessarily living better.

In this century democratic and socialist governments have found ways for the poor to share the benefits of better health. Medicare and Medicaid assumed America's elderly health-care burden. For a time, carefree retirement was a possibility. Then profound change in demographics and rising health-care costs swamped the system. In 1988, for example, the per capita cost for health services in the United States was $2,124. Payments for health services consume an ever greater share of personal income and increasingly exceed the resources of individuals, employers and governments.

What is the outcome of all this? The poor tend not to seek early treatment because of cost. This results in their requiring more extensive and expensive care later on. There is a quadrupling of charges for institutional care which has paralleled the astronomical increase in the numbers of the retired elderly. Age slows recovery from illness and thus requires a disproportionate share of resources for health care.

Medicare is available and provides acute care benefits for those past 65. Medicaid provides chronic and custodial care in institutions, but only if one is virtually destitute. The average annual cost of a nursing home bed is more than $25 thousand. The average individual will exhaust his or her entire life's savings within 13 weeks following admission to a nursing home. The bankrupt individual is then qualified for care in a Medicaid program. Presently, Medicaid covers only 45 percent of nursing home costs. The remainder is assumed by private funds, and monies from insurance and state sources.

Today, the care for the chronically ill and disabled is provided by instituttions. Many patients currently in nursing homes could have remained at home, or could return home, if they had the help needed or the means to pay for it. A 1990 survey of one community showed that for every individual currently in a nursing home there were three individuals with the same need or greater receiving long-term care at home. Many community assistance programs, such as Home Health Nursing, Homemaker Services, Meals on Wheels, Adult Care, Respite Care, Hospice programs, home modification programs, telephone reassurance and transportation programs enable many of the elderly poor to continue independent living and to retain control over their lives.

Our American health care system focuses upon restoring health after it has been lost, and that is very expensive. Hospital care does improve survival time for individuals, but this has very little impact upon life expectancy statistics. The key to long life and good health is not found in a hospital, or even in a doctor's office. Instead, it is found in the realm of our own personal actions— our self-destructive behavior and self-indulgence.

Life shortening diseases are linked to such personal habits as over-eating, smoking, high fat and sugar intake, malnutrition and lack of exercise. The primary reason a patient must have a long hospital stay is for treatment of cardiovascular disease. The second greatest need for the use of hospital bed-days is for the treatment of injuries and burns. Usually, these are the the result of an accident or an act of violence. The use of drugs, alcohol, smoking, careless driving and the failure to use seat belts are all personal habits detrimental to health. It is said that one seat belt is worth a thousand orthopedic surgeons. But it is of no use if you don't buckle it. Your continued good health is your personal responsibility.

Present political and economic reality has shattered the retirement dreams of most Americans. Instead of security, many retired elderly find themselves living below the poverty level. Some can no longer afford to live in the homes they own. Many find themselves in an old familiar rut — pinching pennies to get by today so that we will have enough left for tomorrow. Instead of living on Easy Street off of our hardearned investments, America's elderly are forced to sell assets or seek part-time jobs to meet rising inflation or skyrocketing hospital costs.

It would be helpful to know the limits of life expectancy. On average we will live for three quarters of a century. One authority says that we double our chance of dying every seven years. Theoretically, the human life span is between 100 and 110 years. Some authorities even claim that 150 years is a very real possibility. Not many will make it, however.

At present, America has about 13 thousand centenarians. In 1973, a Russian died who was said to be 168-years-old. He was survived by five living generations and a widow of 120. They had been married for 102 years. The oldest documented American died in 1925 at the age of 111. And Grandma Moses made it to 101.

I don't believe any of these unusual people used an anti-age pill, or that the Russians have a fountain of youth. But I do believe that they must have had something beyond financial security that not only contributed to their longevity but also made those extra years worth living. A clue to that ingredient came to me when I visited a relative nearing 90. I asked why she did not consider moving into a nearby senior retirement center. She replied, "The elderly are my peers and I have found in their segregation they become rather dull. I like to be with young folk. I'm alone in my apartment, but every day I mix with interesting people who are friendly and helpful."

I discovered the same outlook in an archaeological museum. It had been written on a clay tablet six centureis before Christ. The translation was worded: "The mother of Nabadedus affirms the moon god kept me alive for 104 happy years. My eyesight was good, my hearing excellent, my hands and feet were sound, my words well chosen. Food and drink agreed with me. My health was fine and my mind happy. I saw my grandchildren up to the fourth generation in good health and I had my fill of old age."

Perhaps in giving over to government the responsibility for our retirement security we have focused too narrowly upon financial. It is the social aspects of living beyond our productive years that gives life its meaning. To have fun just watching the human drama you must have a seat in the front row with the grandchildren.

President Harry Truman telephoned Herbert Hoover to congratulate him upon his 79th birthday. As he hung up the phone, the feisty Democrat remarked, "That old Republican is lonesome; he needs something to do." Hoover was a humanitarian as well as an engineer. He had always been busy. In China he had worked on flood control and famine relief. He did a repeat performance in the United States after a devastating Mississippi River flood. His abilities were utilized in Europe to ameliorate the devastation and hunger in the wake of two World Wars. President Truman placed him at the head of a new Hoover Commission to suggest ways for reorganizing the federal government. After two years, over 75 percent of the commission's recommendations were implemented, resulting in more efficient government.

Retirement for some busy people can be devastating. Our society judges a person's worth by the job he holds. To awake one morning with no place to go and realize that the world is spinning along quite well without your push is a blow to the ego. The separation from former associates brings on a fitful state of loneliness and depression. Society is not supportive of older individuals who are no longer "productive."

In past agricultural societies, a multigenerational family and a close-knit community gave individuals the sense of belonging. Age dictated a shift in duties, but it never cut one off from others. Rather, the elders of the group were honored and respected.

Most of us do not have irreplaceable abilities, nor do we have a perceptive president to set tasks before us. Therefore we are thrown upon our own resources to find ways to make retirement meaningful. For some, engrossing hobbies or travel suffice. Others require the rejuvenating experience of being needed by someone. Every community has many tasks left undone because they are considered too expensive or not as important as others. These tasks must be tackled by volunteers. Many who have volunteered to help others discover a rejuvenating experience of being needed by someone. Helping others is a most rewarding and meaningful experience. Try it—volunteer for something.

Present society forces us to feel old and useless. Katherine Hepburn expressed it well in a recent interview.

"It is so endless to be old," she said. "Really, it's a bore for anyone with half a brain. But you have to face it and how you do it is a challenge."

Our challenge is to rise above the old-age stereotype. We "old" are a major human resource possessing experience and learned expertise of great societal value. Seniors must encourage the formation of an "age-irrelevant" society, one without arbitrary constraints based on age. Each individual needs opportunities consonant with the abilities they still possess. Involuntary age segregation should not be tolerated. We who find it repugnant to think of ourselves and other seniors as "old" must impart new meaning to out-worn designations.

• • • •

Retirement

Death and taxes, some wise person once said, are the only certainties of human existence. Now a third must be added for those who live long enough: retirement. It is regrettable that many look upon retirement with the same distaste they accord the other two. Retirement, as a new beginning, holds so many opportunities for growth, development, challenge and adventure. But for retirement to be both happy and rewarding, one must have adequate finances and good health.

Our generation has played a part in shaping a society that is extremely harsh to live in when one is both old and poor. Too often today the family is fragmented, forcing its elderly members to rely more and more upon fixed and dwindling resources.

Adequate finances in retirement depends either upon continued income or sufficient savings—and usually both. With retirement, some seniors discover that their newly gained freedom is shackled by a lack of money. And more often than not, they soon discover that inflation has eaten away at what little savings they were able to stash away during their working years. A Senate Committee on Aging found that the manufacturer's cost on prescription drugs during the 1980s rose 152 percent. This increase was three times the rate of inflation. What is quite astounding is that the top 10 drug companies made an average profit of 15.5 percent. Compare that to the 4.6 percent profit made by all the *Fortune 500* companies. Higher property assessments coupled with the increased cost of maintenance for an older home, scuttles the plans of many of the elderly, sending them in desperate search for more affordable housing.

To put it simply, what this all comes down to is that seniors can't afford to be sick. That's why it's both important and smart to have a preretirement physical examination. This will also give you the opportunity to correct any problems you may have while you have health insurance. If surgery is needed it should be done when the cost is shared with your employer. Plus, if you are able to continue medical insurance coverage into retirement, do so.

Everyone needs a meaningful existence, a reason for living. Upon retirement this is found through family and friends. And it is often found in tasks that challenge one's own abilities and use of time.

Retired people sometimes let their minds turn them into semi-invalids. They become frustrated with a "nothingness" retirement. They fear tomorrow and worry about catastrophic illnesses. Although most people will never have a "disaster" illness, the best way to become ill is to think about the possibility that you might.

Mind induced ailments are pretended and/or exaggerated illnesses. Subconsciously, they are used to gain attention. Association with similarly obsessed seniors leads to reinforcement and introversion. Such sick-fests are often a source of improper medication. Comparison tales lead to friendly recommendations. All too often a suggested medication doesn't fit what ails you. Get the facts first, and get them from a reliable medical source. Not only will you have the appropriate medication, but you will gain peace of mind as well.

In socialist countries the basic needs of food, shelter and health are supposed to be met by government. Under such a system, men can retire at age 60 and women at age 55. Women with large families can retire earlier. In former Soviet Russia, men and women continued to work 10 or more years past the age of retirement. The reason was simple—the need for retirement income. Retirement income only assures a marginal existence. In addition, the Russian worker traditionally had little to fulfill him or herself in retirement. There were no senior centers, no special social clubs, and few churches. There were "homes" for the disabled, but no retirement housing. Travel was restricted by permits and was very expensive. Retirement in a socialist country promised a very drab existence.

Given the means, retirement for Americans can be wonderful—that is, of course, if one also has good health. Poor health is not only incapacitating, but it can also reduce us to poverty. Thus, it may additionally deprive us of our independence because of the spiraling costs of medical care.

• • • •

Survival

In 1802 philosopher William Paley wrote:

"Nightly rest and daily bread, the ordinary use of our limbs, and senses, and understandings, are gifts which admit of no comparison with any other."

In those times, pristine though they seemed, only persons of some wealth could be assured of such "gifts." In old age, the poor were dependent upon charity for food, clothing, shelter and medical care. Charity came from family, from neighbors, from the family doctor and from institutions of local government. Today, your health in retirement is largely of your own making. It is a personal responsibility.

You must start to get ready for retirement when you're young. Vital health in retirement is the result of good health practices learned in youth. In retirement you'll reap the benefits from years of good nutrition and a life of moderation. The adjacent states, Nevada and Utah, provide good examples of this. Both states are very much alike except for the difference in life style of their inhabitants. While Nevadans focus on games of chance, momentary thrills and having a good time, Utah inhabitants are more sedate and largely regulated by the Mormon Church. Nevada's death rate is 50 percent greater than the death rate in Utah.

Too many people act as though a bad statistical probability only applies to others and not to themselves. This belief is a comfort to soldiers in battle, criminals, and drivers who don't wear seat belts. None of these people could continue their activity if they did not look on the sunny-side of chance. "Misfortune will only happen to the other guy, but not to me," is their credo. Such thinking is also a solace to those who continue living habits which increase the likelihood of sickness, accidents, disability and death.

Our bodies undergo two changes which seem to be the result of the aging process. First, there is a reduction of our reserve capacity. Most obvious is loss of strength, agility and stamina. Less obvious are the physiologic changes which render the elderly less able to recover from injury and illness. Because healing is slower, it makes good sense to have elective surgery or repair done at a younger rather than at an older age.

A second characteristic of aging is our diminished ability to adapt to change. The elderly have greater difficulty in adjusting to environmental variations. They are also more disturbed by social changes going on about them. We cling to the familiar and find security in routine. To venture into new fields is the province of the young because the inexperience of youth discovers everything to be new. To them, one path looks as good as another. Experience teaches caution, so seniors hesitate to stray too far from the familiar. Among retired elderly, even unfamiliar surroundings can be devastating.

Learning to adjust to the new or unexpected is a skill that can only be mastered by going through the process. All stages of a person's life has problems: joys, fears, potentials. Seek to find a use for what you have attained in a lifetime of learning. The process, of course, will be greatly helped by your mental attitude.

The most helpful mental attitude is happy anticipation. Make plans to do something you think you would enjoy doing. Approach every new activity as an adventure. How often have you longed to do something if you only had the time? Want to get that college degree? All things are possible for those who strive and work to achieve their goal. Reflection and observation come from having lived a life of varied experiences. Now, in retirement, you have the time. So dust off some of those long dormant wishes and see if they can't be fitted into your retirement picture.

Aging is often viewed as a mechanical process. Like a machine, our bodies wear out with age. Vital forces get used up. The battery runs down. One must rest to save dwindling energy. Slow down. These are truisms, but only to a limited degree. Joints, for example do become damaged as the result of wear and tear. Life expectancy is reduced as a result of "burning the candle at both ends." Excessive stress can exceed the body's physical capacity to respond.

Instead of a mechanical machine, we should think of the body as a biological unit. It is self regulating and can grow to build back what has been used up. It can heal itself. It improves skills through use. Strength and endurance come only from greater activity. Dis*use* leads to deterioration. In an experiment, healthy rats were kept immobile over a period of time. Within 21 days, 40 percent were dead A second group was also kept immobile, but was allowed 30 minutes of activity each day. These rats had only a 6 percent mortality rate. Great benefit can be derived from even a little daily physical activity.

From a biological point of view, we rust out rather than wear out. Nobody dies of old age. One dies from a specific cause or disease. There is a biologic malfunction. For you to have survived until now means you must have been endowed with a superior constitution. Good health is the same thing at all ages. Poor health should never be ascribed to the fullness of years. Correcting the underlying cause of poor health will restore function and your capabilities.

· · · ·

Talking With Doctors

As interns, young doctors apply their book learning to the practical care of patients under the guidance of experienced physicians. In my time, no intern discussed or received instructions concerning a patient in the patient's presence, unless the patient was anesthetized. It was believed that truth would upset the patient or belie the physician's mystique. I recall a doctor who was different. Instead of talking to the intern, he explained things to his patient. He would tell his patients' about the treatment he proposed, what he hoped it would accomplish and the chances for a successful result. At the time I believed that patients would be frightened when told of a possible complication or failure. Instead, when an unhappy result occurred, patients felt that their condition might have been a great deal worse had not their smart, wonderful doctor been fully aware of that possibility.

There was a further benefit from full disclosure. The well informed patient could participate in his own healing. This shared responsibility for achieving good health is most advantageous in chronic diseases. Educated patients reduce their dependence upon their physician. Thus, they gain greater freedom and lower medical expenses. Diabetics often become more expert about their disease than many doctors.

As consumers of medical care, patients have the right to know about any treatment that's given them. This applies to medicines prescribed as well as to operations. Ask questions and don't be turned off when the doctor replies, "let me worry about that." It is your disease and it is your worry more than anyone' else's. Busy doctors forget that some oldsters have difficulty in hearing, understanding or remembering instructions. Illness, and even the prescribed medication, can dull one's wits. You should insist that you be given *written* instructions on when and how to take your medication. After you have left the doctor's office, following his instructions becomes your responsibility. Studies have shown that the single most common cause for a drug's ineffectiveness and harmful results was because the patient failed to take the medication properly.

• • • •

Taking Medication

When taking medication several times a day, it is important to take it at the proper time. One can easily forget that a pill may already have been taken and then take a second. Overdosing is most common at bedtime when one is drowsy. It is good practice to count out and set aside a day's number of pills. Mistakes are minimized when you are able to count the remaining pills each time you take medicine.

Time and frequency of medication is gauged by its effect in the body. Vitamins, minerals and hormones are slow acting and have an effect over a long period. With these, precise timing or missing a dose is not important. On the other hand antibiotics must be taken in a manner to produce a high and constant blood level. Some medications are prescribed to suppress or stimulate certain bodily functions. They should be taken at the time their effect is needed.

Many medications work rapidly. Others, like the diuretics, should be taken early in the day so that sleep will not be disturbed. If given with food, most medicine is absorbed more slowly and for a longer period than when taken on an empty stomach. Digestion will destroy some medications and these are either held in the mouth or swallowed in a coated form. Coated and slow release tablets or capsules should never be crushed or broken. This could either destroy their effect or result in an overdose from rapid absorption.

The effect of a potent drug can be modified by another medication taken at the same time. Thus aspirin will augment the effect of anti-coagulants (blood thinners), while vitamin K and liver counteract to increase blood clotting. Alcohol should not be used when taking tranquilizers or anti-depressants. Combined actions on the nervous system could be fatal. Some foods interact with certain medications. Thus persons taking some medications for high blood pressure or severe depressive states should avoid cheese, Chianti wine, pickled herring, yogurt and foods prepared with meat tenderizer.

Ask your doctor to prescribe the cheaper and just as effective generic drug if there is one. He should direct the pharmacist to place the name of the drug on the prescription label. This is doubly important should you travel. Color and shape have little to do with therapeutic effect, and too often "look-alikes" get mixed up and are taken by mistake. You can't be too careful when your health is at stake.

2 HEALTH MENACES

Air Pollution

Urbanization concentrates air pollution so that it becomes harmful to our health. The word "smog"—a mixture of smoke and fog — was coined in 1905 to describe the atmospheric condition over British industrial towns when more than 1,000 deaths occurred in a single episode. The National Clean Air Act was enacted in 1968 to reduce air pollution by chemicals, hydrocarbons and particulates.

After the first 10 years of the act, it was estimated that cleaner air was saving 14,000 lives annually. The dollar cost of reducing industrial and automobile emissions has now prompted Congress to contemplate weakening of the law. But the growing number of elderly need the protection provided by the Clean Air Act.

The air we breathe is a common, God-given resource. We take its purity for granted. When industry continues to pollute our air with their unwanted wastes, our common resource is degraded. The Tacoma Smelter, for example, operated five years under a variance. It poured 15 tons of sulfur oxide into the air each hour. It is assumed that sufficient dilution renders toxic material harmless. This is only partially true. Long exposure to apparently innocuous concentrations of toxic material can have a cumulative harmful effect. The elderly are the segment of the population who have lived long enough to have absorbed significant levels of toxins from many years of exposure. Seniors are the ones who have been incrementally poisoned and some of us die when there is a smog alert.

With advancing age, we become more susceptible to environmental injury because we have no reserve vital capacity. Years ago, when tuberculosis was prevalent, a patient might lose an entire lung. A young person could compensate for this loss because he had sufficient capacity left in the remaining lung. An older person has no such excess capacity. Seniors, with lips already blue from cyanosis, find that even a slight diminution of air quality has a significant effect upon health

Do you recall President Reagan's physician remarking upon the President's unusually rapid recovery from an assassin's bullet? His rapid recovery is the more surprising when one remembers that over half of the men born in 1911 were already dead. Pope John Paul's low grade fever would be considered medically insignificant except for the fact that he is over 60. Age slows healing. Old lungs with emphysema are inefficient at best; they can be further impaired by any degradation in the air they breathe.

Everyone agrees that carbon monoxide from

automobile exhaust is deadly when confined within a closed garage. It is no less poison when released on our city streets. Hemoglobin in red blood cells have a greater and more lasting affinity for carbon monoxide than it does for oxygen. Brief exposure to carbon monoxide appears harmless if an individual has an excess of hemoglobin. But the elderly are often anemic and have no such excess. Additionally, the elderly are usually pedestrians. To climb our hilly streets they must breathe deeply. They endure long waiting at crosswalks while idling cars pour more carbon monoxide into the walled-in confines of city streets. The walking elderly are the most susceptible segment of the population to air contamination. They are delicate like the canaries once carried into mines to check the air quality. The continued good health of seniors depends upon clean air.

• • • •

Pure Water

> *"It's a great place to visit, but don't drink the water!"*
> —Travel Agent.

Bad water has traditionally been associated with "travelers' diarrhea." Without doubt, the British habit of drinking tea contributed greatly to Britain's success in building an empire. Tea can be prepared only by boiling water, and boiled water is sterile.

Modern bacteriology provides evidence that disease often comes from contaminated water. The earliest demonstration occurred when a cholera epidemic in Hamburg, Germany, was traced to drinking water from the Elbe River. Cholera vibrio reached the Elbe because the river was used to carry away the city sewage. Major population centers were quick to learn from the Hamburg experience. Chlorination to sterilize drinking water is now universal.

The World Health Organization (WHO) has played a major role in helping to globalize this simple lesson. WHO is one of many cooperative endeavors of the United Nations that has contributed to better living throughout the world. It has made possible pure, municipal water supplies in almost every place that a tourist is likely to visit. The travel agent is wrong. *We can drink the water!*

Yet, travelers' diarrhea continues to be a tourist hazard. Visitors in Chicago became ill with amoebic dysentery. Yes, this happened in smart, modern Chicago, a city whose chlorinated drinking water comes from Lake Michigan. Sewage leaves via the Chicago river. The river water no longer runs into the lake but carries sewage down the Mississippi. How could tropical amoebic dysentery occur in such a modern metropolis? Bacteriologists traced the Chicago epidemic to contaminated salad greens served in swank hotel dining rooms. When traveling, be wary of uncooked foods and unsanitary food handlers, and don't forget to wash your own hands before eating. You will thus avoid the way most Americans contract travelers diarrhea.

But there is an alarming new chapter on the relationship of drinking water to disease, one that involves some of the nation's most highly industrialized centers.

The usual method of water purification is chlorination. Most people know this already. Chlorine kills disease bacteria and makes water "safe" to drink. For many years industries have dumped chemical wastes into nearby lakes and streams. These chemicals have become concentrated in our great river systems like the Mississippi and the Hudson. Recent findings have shown that chlorine reacts with many of these waste chemicals to form chlorinated compounds. The ingestion of these chlorinated compounds has proven to cause cancer. The point to be made here is that it may sometimes be wise to follow the advice of the travel agent. And even if you don't travel, you may still want to work for the safe and proper disposal of industrial wastes.

• • • •

Arsenic

Napoleon Bonaparte died before he was 52. His death, in 1821, was attributed to cancer of the stomach, but his final illness remains shrouded in mystery. His familiar pose with his hand inside his shirt was an affectation, not because he was holding a painful stomach. Napoleon's poor health coincided with the arrival of a new British governor to his island prison of St. Helena. With the governor's arrival, however, there were episodes of upset stomach and a loss of appetite. Where Napoleon had once been a strong, vigorous and healthy leader, he now had intermittent fevers, a pallid and sallow complexion and an enlarged liver. His doctor suspected cirrhosis. Napoleon charged that he was "surrounded by paid assassins" and became a recluse, never leaving the house on St. Helena's in his last three years.

Taken together, all these symptoms, including the mental change, are suggestive of chronic arsenic poisoning. Even the terminal cancer can be attributed to the now known carcinogenic affect of arsenic. Arsenic has been a favorite poison throughout history because it imparts no taste, odor or color to arouse suspicion. Analysis of Napoleon's hair showed 10.3 parts per million of arsenic. Tests of hair sections indicate that poisoning was intermittent. But still we can't be sure that arsenic was given to him with homicidal intent. It could have been prescribed by the doctor as a tonic or for treatment of amoebic intestinal parasites. Or perhaps Napoleon was accidentally poisoned in the same manner as a recent American Ambassador to Italy. Arsenic was traced from the Ambassador's food to old paint crumbling and dropping from the ceiling.

Arsenic is an unusual mineral producing different effects in different people. It is the active ingredient in commercial products sold for the purpose of killing insects, vegetation, rodents or other animals. Yet Swiss Alpine climbers are said to eat small amounts of the chemical to improve their strength and stamina. A little in poultry feed causes faster and greater growth in chickens.

Perhaps the chickens benefit by the elimination of their parasites in the same manner that plants grow more lush when arsenic pesticides sterilize their soil and foliage. Commercially, arsenic is useful to the ceramic, glass, wall paper, paint and pharmaceutical industries. There are thousands of arsenic compounds which differ widely in their toxicity to humans. Careless use of agricultural products is the usual source of arsenic poisoning.

A closed copper smelter in Tacoma spewed arsenic into the air for 80 years during the smelting process. The smelter's tall stack lifted emissions high enough into the atmosphere to ensure wide dispersal of its poisonous fumes. This diluted the immediate toxic fallout of the chemical in surrounding communities. But today, dangerous concentrations of poison are still found in the air and soil within a radius of 12 miles of the copper smelter.

Slag containing arsenic was once used in our roads, although that is no longer done. When that was the practice, however, there was always the possibility that road dust could spread the hazard. Rain also leached the arsenic from the roads and soil, carrying it into surface water and the underlying aquifer. In consequence of this, arsenic has concentrated in local commercial plants and animals, making them unsuitable for human consumption.

Scientists can't agree on the health hazard of small amounts of arsenic ingested over a long period of time. Perhaps small amounts improve tolerance because some smelter workers seem to be unharmed by quantities that are lethal to someone who has never been exposed to the chemical. Tolerance is affected by many factors which mediate the body's ability to detoxify arsenic and excrete it. A fever, when caused by riboflavin deficiency, can reduce arsenic tolerance by as much as 50 percent. But this relates only to arsenic's toxicity, not its carcinogenicity. Arsenic-caused cancers are chiefly of the lungs, skin and liver.

Smelter workers have three times the lung cancer of workers in other industries. Studies indicate that arsenic augments cancer generated by other substances as well. Cancer from smoking, for example, is more likely when there is also an arsenic pesticide residue in the tobacco or in the air. Seniors are a sensitive population for cancer because carcinogens usually take a very long time to produce cancer. With so many other known cancer-causing chemicals turning up in our food, water and air, it would seem prudent to restrict arsenic emissions from all sources to the lowest possible level.

. . . .

Carcinogens

Cancer is the plague of our generation. Just in our lifetime, cancer rose from eighth to second place among the most common causes of death. It accounts for about one out of every five deaths in America. Yet such statistics alone do not tell the whole story. With modern treatment, many people recover from cancer and die from other causes. The average cost to treat each cancer case has continued its rise above $10,000, but over the years the rate of success has improved very little.

Some types of cancer seem to vary according to nationality. Scots, for example, have the highest rate of lung cancer. It is twice that of American men and seven times the rate of men from Portugal. American Blacks have the highest incidence of prostate cancer, eight times that of the Japanese. Japan can claim the least breast cancer. Leading the world in breast cancer is the Netherlands, where it occurs six times as often as it does anywhere else. Japan has more cancer of the stomach, about eight times the rate of the United States.

Cancer appears to be related to geography. When people migrate to a different country, their type of cancer and its frequency tends to adjust to that of the country to which they move. Probably 70 percent to 90 percent of all cancer is caused by factors found in the environment.

The National Cancer Institute and the Public Health Service mapped American cancer mortality by counties. Those counties having chemical plants, oil refineries, asbestos works, metal mining, processing and smelting tend to have the highest cancer rates.

Salem County, New Jersey, leads the 3,056 counties of the nation. In Salem County 25 percent of the male population was employed in the chemical industry. But women and men otherwise employed also had a high rate of cancer. Chemical wastes were being vented into the atmosphere where they were dispersed and diluted to a point considered harmless. Chemical wastes were also flushed away into a nearby body of water. Some were buried in dumps where rain leached out the chemicals and carried them into the aquifer. It was concluded that cancer-causing substances were escaping from the chemical plant into the environment to injure everyone in the county.

Waste disposal methods are inadequate and hazardous. Consider what has happened during the 20th century. Oil refining, by cracking, gave the chemical industry a new set of building blocks, enabling it to develop organic chemical products that never existed previously. Nature has yet to learn how to handle many of them. Biologic processes made the old organic substances biodegradable, but plastics are another matter. Some of these new substances have been found to cause cancer. They are called carcinogens. When carcinogens are also fat soluble, they accumulate in animal fat and concentrate in our food chain.

Tacoma may seem a long way from New Jersey, but we have problems similar to those of Salem County. In September of 1981, fat soluble organic chemical carcinogens were found by the Health Department in a city well. Investigation determined that the chemical was leached by rain from contaminated property abandoned 30 years earlier. The municipal underwater aquifer lies 200 feet below the surface contamination. Usually water is pumped from this well for about three months each summer to supplement Tacoma's potable water supply. No longer can it be used for domestic purposes. The concentration of carcinogens is so great that the water may not even be dumped into Commencement Bay. The amount of carcinogens in the aquifer is unknown. It is theorized that the chemical was dumped before anyone suspected that the chemicals might get into the water or cause cancer. Tacoma built five 40-foot tall "stripping" towers. These will remove carcinogens from the water, transferring them to the air for dilution and dispersion. Hopefully, this will end it. But there are other sources of Tacoma's cancer plague that are not so easily identified. We have a real problem.

A 1992 study by researchers in Hartford seems to have uncovered the link between manufactured chemicals and breast cancer. Their evidence is that cancerous breast tissue from 40 women contained twice the amount of fat soluble carcinogens found in a comparable group of normal women. Polychlorinated biphenols (PCB) are used in the electronic industry and dichlorodiphenyl-dichloroethylene (DDE), is a byproduct of the pesticide DDT. These chemicals store in body fat, do not readily break down in nature and can be passed from animal to animal through the food chain and mother's milk. Pollutants expelled into the environment 50 years ago continue to pose a danger. Over 2 billion tons of these substances have been used by the pesticide and electronic industries since 1929. None of the women who had cancer were exposed to PCBs or DDE on industrial jobs. It is therefore concluded that chemicals were picked up from contaminated food, water or air

A larger-scale study is to be funded by the National Cancer Institute.

• • • •

Radiation

X rays and radium were first used in medicine shortly after 1900. The radiation was called "X" because it was an unknown quantity. The new technology spread to the public sector and was even used to fit shoes. X rays and radium were not only applied to cure cancer, but were popular "cures" for arthritis and the "rejuvenation" of the elderly.

Then the bubble burst. Workers painting luminous numbers on watch faces developed leukemia. Doctors making fluoroscopic examinations lost their fingers and developed cancer. These delayed effects from radiation are now well known and avoided.

X ray and atomic particles carry a great deal of energy that is released upon their striking an object. It is like sunlight streaming through cold air and outer space to warm your hand. When sufficient energy is focused upon a cancer cell, the cell will be destroyed. Normal cells through which radiation must pass may not be killed, but they are frequently altered by radiation. Cellular disorganization from radiation may later turn normal cells into cancer.

Radium, cobalt and X-ray radiation treatment aim to kill individual cancer cells that can spread malignant growth to other body parts. Since normal cells are also injured by radiation, dosage is carefully monitored and directed to affect mainly the rapidly growing cancer cells. Other body areas are shielded. Cancer is attacked from several directions by rotation of either the machine or the patient. Treatment must be interrupted to allow intervals for recovery of normal cells and the patient.

Despite all efforts to protect them, patients get radiation sickness. The skin surface becomes red and painful, as from sunburn. Hair falls out. Anemia follows the decreased production of red blood cells. The number of white blood cells may be knocked too low to fight infection. Blood platelets can diminish to the point that bleeding occurs. Absorption of cells killed by radiation causes fever like a chronic abscess or gangrene. There is no appetite — you "feel rotten." Many people become extremely nauseated and vomit. No one would wish radiation sickness on his worst enemy, yet it is given to the ones we love when necessary.

· · · ·

Finance

In 1983 the Institute for Research on Poverty completed a study on the relative economic status of the aged. It concluded that, on average, the aged are no more likely to be poor than the non-elderly. The study also found that no category of citizens was more diverse than those who had primarily their longevity in common. The elderly include 60-year-olds playing tennis outside their Sun Belt condominiums, as well as the nonagenarians barricaded in unheated tenements in the snow belt. To be old and poor is much worse than being just poor because the old cannot work to improve their lot. They have outlived their friends and they are more likely to need medical care.

One of the research findings was that elderly

couples and most women need less money to obtain the same standard of living as a household
headed by a man at any age. It is believed that those
who manage on less do so through personal auster-
ity and greater efficiency. Retirees are more likely
to have durable assets, reducing the cost of living.
For example, residing in one's own home can be
less costly than renting.

We commonly assume that people save during
their working years so that they may spend during
retirement to maintain their superior standard of
living. This idea is not borne out by the study.
Examination of income and consumption levels indicates that the elderly actually save significantly
more of their lower income than the non-elderly.
Surprisingly, the oldest appear to save the most.
The researchers admit that their data does not include persons who failed to save enough when
young and therefore do not maintain an independent household. People, young or old, without
money never become savers.

It has been suggested that the elderly save
because they have lost mobility and health. Both
characteristics are required for the purchase and
enjoyment of consumer goods. There may be other
contributing factors as well.

Seniors who have detached themselves from
the world have few wants. Saving behavior can
result from a deeply felt insecurity. Children of the
depression revert to frugal habits when facing uncertain circumstances or indefinite life span. They

have watched inflation erode their savings. The immediate future is unpredictable. Health and strength are fading. They have no wish to become burdens on either their relatives or the state. What is "squandered" today will not be there for that hour of need which may come with every, tomorrow.

Yet excessive frugality may set the stage for the ill health the elderly so greatly fear. A senior bragged that he had spent less than $20 for groceries over a two week period. Poor nutrition results from lack of variety and quality in the foods we consume. Foods high in sugar and starch are relatively cheap and easy to prepare. However, they generally are low in nutritive and health preserving vitamins, minerals, protein and fiber content. Fresh fruits, vegetables, meat, eggs and milk are more expensive but well worth the greater cost.

Older Americans, rich or poor, can stretch dollars and thus improve their living conditions because of many community services. Lower fares and admission prices, discount pharmacies, and medical, housing and meal rates give the elderly an economic advantage. Basically these are attempts to forestall a much more expensive social alternative, the nursing home.

Community services available in most communities will help your dollars go further.

3

ADJUSTING TO PROBLEMS

Forgetfulness

Dear Aunt Abby:

I'm sorry to hear that Uncle Ben is beginning to show his age. People seldom realize that they are changing. We are aware when older folk become forgetful, confused and less able to cope, but we just never believe it can happen to us.

Doctors don't know the precise cause for forgetfulness, or aging for that matter. They do know, however, that when brain cells die they are not replaced. Accumulated injuries throughout our lifetime take their toll. In time the cerebral deficits caused by the whacks we've taken can become quite significant.

Everyone recognizes a stroke that paralyzes its victim. We know it is produced by circulatory failure in the motor area of the brain where movement is controlled. The motor area comprises only a tiny part of the entire brain, which is similarly affected by circulatory changes. "Silent" strokes occurring in other parts will knock out our "computer" or "memory" storage. Loss of these areas may result in cognitive deficits and personality changes.

Large constricted arteries can sometimes be opened to give better brain circulation. Drug treatment with cerebral stimulants or psychic energizers, however, are not always helpful. Psychiatry is not applicable since it requires understanding and the cooperation of the patient.

Senility is called our second childhood for good reason: It is a state of dependance. Like a child, Uncle Ben will be more secure when he is guided by daily routines in familiar surroundings. He can be helped to find purpose and satisfactions in his life. He will have a difficult time trying to concentrate and remember, so it is natural that his responses will be uncertain and slow. How fortunate he is to have you there to depend upon.

Your loving nephew

•   •   •   •

Alzheimer's Disease

Forgetting to Remember? Do you find it increasingly difficult to remember names and facts? Advancing age is an acceptable excuse. Most of us sometimes grope for what was once "on the tip of the tongue." Of course, we never recall some things, like our social security number or the date of the Magna Carta. Perhaps we never knew them in the first place, or we may have seldom used them. Some seniors, however, have trouble remembering their own addresses and telephone numbers. A few may even remember events that never happened.

Alzheimer's disease affects about one in 20 people 65 and over. It strikes 10 percent of people who are over the age of 75. Memory loss can come from head injury or a stroke. Fever, infection, alcohol and drugs can also cause amnesia and disorientation. But these memory losses have an organic origin and will usually disappear when the cause is removed. No cause is known for Alzheimer's disease and the condition simply grows worse as time goes on.

Some seniors are thought to have Alzheimer's disease when they merely suffer from sensory deprivation. Usually these people live alone and cut themselves off from society. Some become mentally and emotionally isolated because of excessive or inappropriate medication. These elderly are like Rip Van Winkle—once they reawaken to human contact they're restored to normal.

Outwardly, the Alzheimer's patient appears normal. Confusion and agitation happens primarily at night. He may become unreasonably obstinate and excessively critical. At the same time he may be completely unaware of the consequences of his actions. Many never realize that they are a problem. Resentment may be the response to guidance and simple requests. The only certainty about Alzheimer's is that it will cause unforeseen problems and the caretaker will need help.

Spouses are likely to feel that they should

bear the entire burden of care for their partner. This expectation is unrealistic and may be disadvantageous to both patient and caretaker. Community services should be called upon to relieve and share the continuous and mounting pressure of responsibility. In many communities there are consulting services and support groups eager to help. Use them. Such programs as Chore Services, Day Care Centers, Meals on Wheels and Visiting Nurse are there to lend a hand and to help assume some of the routine tasks of caretaker.

Does your own forgetfulness worry you? Could you be a victim of Alzheimer's? Probably not. Forgetting is normal. Even young folks draw a blank from time to time. Forgetting is an aid that helps us adapt to survival demands. How can you learn something new if your mind is cluttered with vivid, unpleasant memories that never fade or go away. The human mind needs to make room for new ideas, new experiences, new plans and new memories.

• • • •

Parkinson's Disease

Among older citizens the most common neurologic disability is Parkinson's disease. It is also called paralysis agitans or shaking paralysis. Pierce County, Wash., has more than 60,000 seniors. Among them about 120 will develop Parkinson's disease this year. About two in every 1,000 above the age of 55 is afflicted with the disease. The affliction carries a mortality rate three times greater than normal. Recent improvements in treatment are very promising.

At the outset of the disease trembling is noted when trying to make precision movements with the hand. Once agile movements are replaced by hesitation. As the disease progresses, each voluntary movement becomes increasingly difficult. Depression grows. Simple tasks like eating, swallowing, washing and dressing become frustrating impossibilities. The body may bow forward, with elbows and knees bent. Walking becomes an off-balance shuffle. There is loss of muscular mobility. The face may change to an expressionless mask. Speech loses force and becomes difficult to understand. Printing may become the only legible form of writing. Weakness may continue to the point of paralysis.

Symptoms of the disease occur because certain nerve cells in the brain fail to produce dopamine. Dopamine is a neurotransmitting substance necessary to energize nerves controlling voluntary muscles. Another enzyme normally destroys dopamine the moment after it performs its function of neurotransmission. This is because continuous neurotransmission, such as occurs with strychnine poisoning, would be undesirable. There must be a balance. Both dopamine and the enzyme are needed in turn.

Dopamine can be taken orally in the form of

L-dopa. Large frequent doses are required since there is no storage, and it is rapidly destroyed by the enzyme. Only a tiny amount from a large dose ever reaches the deficient nerve cells, but it is enough to restore function temporarily. L-dopa slows the progression of Parkinson's disease and cuts mortality by half. With it, most patients are again able to care for themselves — and that is a great blessing. Most persons can adjust to the nausea and the loss of appetite brought on by the large and frequent doses of the medication. Unfortunately, some persons cannot tolerate L-dopa. In certain cases of heart disease, it must not be used. Vitamin B6 also reduces the availability of L-dopa to the nerve cells and should therefore be avoided.

Implanting brain tissue from fetal abortions holds great promise as a permanent source of L-dopa. For the sake of present and future Parkinson victims, let's hope the matter of fetal tissue use can soon be divorced from politics.

Physical therapy techniques should be applied since they may be of great and lasting benefit. Improvement will follow if they are done carefully at home on a daily schedule.

· · · ·

Custodial Care

Independence Day is celebrated by all Americans unless they are felons, the ill or the failing elderly. Law-breakers forfeit their right to freedom. The sick and elderly are unable to exercise their right because they must physically rely upon others. The elderly were once young, sound and independent. They saved to prepare for their retirement years. Many are disappointed today to discover that their savings have been eaten away by inflation. They can no longer afford the basic needs to survive, such as food, clothing, shelter and health maintenance. Where can they turn for assistance?

In developing nations, large families are appreciated because they are a form of social security. Families take care of their handicapped and aging relatives. In America, on the other hand, social security is often considered to be the government's responsibility. In reality, quite the opposite is true. Relatives continue to provide 80 percent of all long-term care in the home.

We seniors are the tough survivors. We have outlived the other members of our generation. We may be afflicted with chronic diseases which sap our strength, but which generally are not life-threatening. We have also learned to live with some sensory deficits. Perhaps, our "get-up-and-go" has "got-up and went." Even so, we get by until sudden misfortune trips us up. Then we are rushed to the hospital for emergency care and restorative treatment.

Hospitals provide immediate expert therapy, but they are extremely expensive and are not well adapted to care for chronic illnesses. Older patients receive only about one hour of treatment for each day they spend in long-term care in a hospital. Hospitals, for their part, simply provide food, shelter and rest while Nature takes her own time to perform the healing miracle. Some seniors are hospitalized longer because they have no one at home to receive and care for them. And all too often, no convalescent or nursing home beds are available.

Beds are in short supply because the older patient has outlived his support network. During convalescence, a support network of family and friends is necessary up to the time the patient is able to resume independent living. It is estimated that 50 percent of people who live in nursing homes are there because they have nowhere else to go. They get "custodial" care, as though they were a piece of furniture, with little help from insurance plans or Medicare. Custodial care has few rewards to make life worth living.

A relative of mine once wrote in response to a suggestion that her husband be placed in a nursing home: "We really appreciate your concern and realize what you are saying has verity, but we don't feel the time has yet come for us to take action. We are doing the one thing of importance to us that no one else has the understanding to perform. We have concern for each other based on long experience in knowing and respecting our different personalities. As long as we have moments of communication, we are luckier than most and what better can we do with our time than spend it in our sylvan hideaway, keeping up with the interests and turmoil of our world through reading, television and the loved ones who let us vicariously enjoy their activities.

"There are frustrations, to be sure, and it is hard to handle the handicaps of decreased energy and limited ability, but a little stress makes you know that you are alive. As long as we have the physical ability to handle our environment, I think the time has not yet come for any change."

Perhaps this devoted wife can make it for a little longer. Many people "burn out" trying to provide unaccustomed care while performing essential daily tasks. Here's a thought: the ill seldom notice their surroundings, but they are acutely aware of any lack of attention. What families should do then is what they do best: talk and visit. The work that assures survival in a home environment would be best borne by the community and social service organizations. Every community has some organizations that provide chore services. Unfortunately, most are underfunded, overworked and rely almost solely upon volunteers. Volunteers can fill the gap in a support network composed of family, friends, neighbors, churches, and social clubs.

Volunteers are a special breed. They freely sacrifice their own independence to serve others. They involve themselves in life-affirming activities as they give willingly of their talents and time to help others remain independent. And even a little independence is worth celebrating.

•   •   •   •

Institutional Insensitivity

When "put away" in an institution, individuals tend to lose their identity as well as their independence. Management efficiency demands conformity and regimentation. A client (patient) subtly becomes re-classified according to disease and place. Too often one ends up as "that old bag with shingles in room 167, bed two." This insensitivity is well illustrated below in the poem, "See Me." The author of this poem is unknown. It is said to have originated in the geriatric ward of Ashludie Hospital, near Dundee, Scotland. It was popularized in Tacoma, Wash., by Chris Powell on the television show "60 MPH" (Making People Happy). The show was produced for the Tacoma-Pierce County Council on Aging by Hal Reinhardt. Carl Seidel was the master of ceremonies.

SEE ME

What do you see, nurses, what do you see?
What are you thinking, when you look at me?
A crabby old woman, not very wise,
Uncertain of habit, with far-away eyes,
Who dribbles her food and makes no reply
When you say in a loud voice "I do wish you'd try."
Who seems not to notice the things that you do
And forever is losing a stocking or shoe.
Who unresisting or not, lets you do as you will
With bathing and feeding, the long day to fill.

Is that what you're thinking, is that what you see
Then open your eyes, nurses,
you're looking at ME.

I'll tell you who I am, as I sit here so still,
As I rise at your bidding and eat at your will.
I'm a small child of ten, with a father and mother,
Brothers and sisters who love one another.
A girl of sixteen with wings on her feet
Dreaming that soon now a lover she'll meet.
A bride soon at twenty — my heart gives a leap
Remembering the vows that I promised to keep;
At twenty-five now I have young of my own
Who need me to build a secure happy home;
A woman of thirty, my young growing fast,
Bound to each other with ties that will last;
At forty my sons have grown and are gone,
But my man's beside me to see I don't mourn;
At fifty once more babes play 'round my knee,
Again we know children, my loved one and me.

Dark days are upon me, my husband is dead,
I look at the future, I shudder with dread,
For my young are scattered, rearing young of their own
And I dream of the years and the love that I've known.
I'm an old woman now and nature is cruel
'Tis her jest to make old age look like a fool.
The body is crumbled, grace and vigor depart,
There's a stone now where once I had heart.

But inside this old carcass a young girl still dwells,
And now and again my battered heart swells.
I remember the joys, I remember the pain,
And I'm loving and living life over again.
I think of the years, all too few - gone too fast,
And I accept the stark fact that nothing can last.
So open your eyes, nurses, open and see,
Not a crabby old woman,   look closer—SEE ME!

• • • •

Behavior

Many birds and animals are territorial by nature. Survival of the individual and the species depends upon each gaining sufficient sustenance from the immediate surroundings. A bird will define its particular territory with a song and some sort of physical display. Animals patrol constantly and mark their borders with bodily scent. When an intruder of the same species encroaches upon a "home" territory, the "owner" displays an assertive pattern of behavior. The battle is chiefly a sham with the invader backing away to continue looking for his own unclaimed territory.

Psychologists compare territorial behavior in birds and animals with certain human characteristics. A meek "Casper Milktoast" will sometimes become a veritable tiger in defense of home or cultural values. Assertive behavior is commonly used to dominate others, and so gain ends with little struggle. Thus, in the nuclear family parents use assertive behavior toward children. Authority expressed in attitude or tone of voice keeps the child in line. But eventually the child needs to become an individual and possess his own "territory" free of adult domination. As the child learns to also be assertive there may be a crisis since each party seeks exclusive control of the identical "territory." The parent must back off or there will be severe damage to family relationships or the child's personality. Grandparents can be helpful catalysts during a child's transition period.

Traditionally, human society has been governed by dominant individuals who have been assertive and aggressive. Within a stratified society, conflict is avoided when there is passive acceptance on the part of the governed. This subject-class "knows its place" and accepts the crumbs from the "territory" of the privileged. But America was founded upon the ideology of equality. Here, no one is more equal than another. That is, of course, the ideal. Women and minorities are learning to be assertive. They claim rights and privileges long assumed to be outside their "territory."

Confrontation by two assertive individuals is often threatening to each and can lead to violence. As a society, we are too prone to use deadly force in settling differences. Here again , seniors, with their experience in living, can be helpful. They can provide alternative solutions that are less harmful to the disputants, and to our society.

On the national scene our elected officials are often all too willing to rely upon assertive and aggressive behavior. They continually look to military solutions on matters that seemingly could be resolved by courtesies and negotiation. They play a game of "chicken" with the lives of the American people. We pay other costs in the form of higher taxes, greater indebtedness, ever rising inflation, and a withering economy. And there is no end in sight. Assertive behavior, for sure, has no place in negotiations that honestly seek solutions to mutual problems. Seniors must advocate the views of world spiritual leaders.

We are told that violence to instill fear is required to force enemy compliance with U.S. wishes. If that is so, compliance is achieved without altering hearts or changing minds. The enemy remains an enemy and bides his time till revenge is possible. No doubt, some people would rather be "dead than red," but there are other choices for those wishing to live. Christians are admonished to seek ways to convert their enemies rather than to die with them.

Territorial behavior by birds and animals serves to preserve their lives. It works. But the concept is irrational and misused when applied to complex human problems.

• • • •

Prolonging Life

> *"For everything there is a season. A time to be born, and a time to die."*
> —Ecclesiastes 3:1-2

The awesome capability of modern medicine poses serious ethical and legal problems for those providing medical care to the elderly. Today, science is able to postpone death far beyond the time that it would come naturally. Doctors define life in purely biological terms—they look for vital signs. But is biological life alone meaningful? The aging Thomas Jefferson wrote of himself, "Bodily decay is gloomy in prospect but of all human contemplations, the most abhorrent is body without mind."

Health Care Providers are facing a Catch 22 dilemma. Will they be criticized because they use "heroic" measures that serve only to prolong dying? Or will they be sued because they did not do everything possible to prolong life? The proper time to "pull the plug" of a life support system is difficult to determine. Sometimes it will only be done by legal authority. The problem becomes more difficult in a crisis when resuscitative efforts have been initiated without full assessment or authority. This situation can arise whenever an ambulance is called to transport a seriously ill or dying person.

Modern ambulances are wonderfully equipped for every conceivable emergency. They can also provide intensive care during transport. The attending medic has been thoroughly trained in the use of every device at his disposal. Not only can he check all the vital signs such as pulse and blood pressure, but he also has a cardiac monitor. He can defibrillate the heart, and maintain a clear airway by suction. He can administer oxygen, intubate and even breathe for the patient. Intravenous fluid can be started with a number of helpful solutions.

The medic is trained to act in a crisis. His purpose is to save life, and he can read the signs of impending death. Yet he may not realize that, for some, dying can be a very slow drawn-out and expensive process. It is very expensive and may be ill-advised to begin intensive crisis care for a person who is terminally ill with cancer, or who is in a coma.

Lifesaving and life-sustaining abilities are necessary and useful. They help the healthy to survive a crisis and go on living to their normal life expectancy. But the elderly, in general failing health, are different. It is sometimes better that they be allowed to die a natural death.

On June 20, 1980, Pope John Paul II said, "It is important to protect at death the dignity of the human person against a technological attitude that threatens to become an abuse."

You can protect yourself by making a "living will." * Talk over your feelings with your friends, relatives and especially your doctor. Then, while

* Please see Appendix for living will model.

you are still of sound mind, make a living will for the future guidance of medical attendants. Call you local Hospice if you want help or more information.

• • • •

Travel Tips

Never before in history have so many traveled so fast and so far. Annually, almost five million Americans visit tropical areas where their health is protected, chiefly by their own individual actions, and good luck to boot. We are seldom aware of the vast hygienic differences between this industrialized nation and Third World countries. Here in the states we are accustomed to safe water, safe food and safe swimming areas. We look at mosquitos, fleas and other insects as minor nuisances that bite, sting and cause itching. In the Third World insects are also carriers of diseases.

Illness is spread to the healthy from persons or animals who are sick or recently recovered from a disease. Knowledge of the way diseases are transmitted will help the traveler use precautionary measures to stay well. Healthy persons contract diseases in the following ways: by direct contact with the ill , or by a person carrying the disease-causing bacteria; by indirect contact with objects handled by the ill person; by insect carriers; and by drinking contaminated water, or eating contaminated food.

Travel preparations will depend upon where you are going and how long you plan to stay. Vaccination and immunization procedure are no longer required by most countries. They are probably not advantageous if your visit will be short and not off the beaten tourist track. However, check with your doctor or the Health Department before you go. If you have health problems, talk your travel plans over with your doctor. Have him give you sufficient medication and instructions on its use in every circumstance. All medicine should be labeled with generic names. They may have to be declared and shown at customs. And perhaps you will require care away from home.

Prepare for the worst. Put together a kit for your own use. It might contain the following items: soap for washing hands; antiseptic wipes (to use when you can't wash); insect repellant; sunscreen to protect from sunburn; antiseptic ointment for minor scratches; band-aids; antihistamine nasal decongestant (this is especially important if you must fly with a cold); Tylenol or aspirin for headache and minor pain; Imodium (over-the-counter medication for diarrhea and cramping).

When venturing to foreign climes, adopt the following procedures. Wash your hands frequently and always before eating. Soap is an effective disinfectant. Eat only well-cooked food and raw fruit and vegetables that you peel yourself. Fresh salads and dairy products are best avoided. Stick to boiled water, tea, coffee, carbonated and alcoholic drinks without ice. Tap water which is too hot to touch is okay for brushing teeth and drinking. Water purification tablets require a long contact time and do not kill encysted parasites in cold water.

Be aware that diarrhea will carry away minerals and water that your body needs. Such a loss can cause serious drug overdosage when you are taking medication for high blood pressure or heart trouble. If you are diabetic, dehydration, vomiting, and even loss of appetite, can have grave consequences.

So explore the world. Visit those "far away places with strange sounding names." Gather a bouquet of lovely memories. But take care that you do not pick up some exotic disease among the fascinating souvenirs you bring back home.

• • • •

Living Poor

" God bless us every one"
—Tiny Tim

Charles Dickens wrote *A Christmas Carol in Prose* for the Christmas of 1843. Like much of his writing, it was critical of society and highlighted the injustices of England's industrial revolution. His readers knew about low wages and a seven-day work week. They accepted the unjust gap between the rich and the poor. Americans today know little of the setting, yet the story continues to have great appeal. The characterization of Ebenezer Scrooge is timeless.

Scrooge was a miserly, ill-tempered, un-friendly "old" buzzard who had a change of heart. Not yet retired, he couldn't have been as old as many of today's seniors. Life expectancy then was scarcely more than 40. His business partner, "old" Marley, had been "dead as a doornail" for seven years. (Dickens himself died at the age of 58.). As an employer, Scrooge was a skinflint. He forced his clerks to work long hours in cold unpleasant conditions for meager wages. His employees received no fringe benefits,not even a Christmas Eve party such as the one hosted by old Master Feziwig. Workers could barely afford the extravagance of celebrating Christmas at home.

Workers in 20th century America are also facing hard times. While the stock market zooms upward, management executives collect astronomical salaries and "perks." Yet, everyday, factories close and the ranks of the unemployed swell. America also has many retired, disabled and elderly who have become impoverished through inflation and ever rising taxes. They, too, must scrimp to meet the minimal costs for such simple essentials as light and heat for their homes. So they reduce spending for clothing, food, dental and health care. There is little else they can do to help themselves. Dickens has a message for America's Scrooges.

Ebenezer Scrooge was unlike most of the

wealthy of his day, or of ours. He wasted no money on himself. One can only wonder what enjoyment he found in living like his impoverished employees. The story recounts that he went home to double lock himself into commodious chambers which were cold, dark and dismal. He huddled before a tiny fire to eat gruel as an evening meal. Scrooge is said to have liked it that way because cold and darkness were cheap, and so was gruel.

There are a few more affluent seniors today who, like Scrooge, spend paltry sums for their daily needs. Miserly, they identify with the destitute while "squirreling away" their fortunes. Their wealth is of benefit to no one. They court malnutrition while living on restricted "mush" diets. They risk hypothermia in their cold homes. They risk injury as they stumble about in darkness. They act in fear of an uncertain future and so die sooner—in poverty. Locked away from a caring world of family and friends, they live a dull existence leading to the "Bah! Humbug!" mentality of a Scrooge.

Dickens' story tells of the change which came over "old man" Scrooge. His personality was changed by visions of Christmas Past, Christmas Present and of Christmas yet to come. Overnight he became receptive to love and affection from other people. In turn, he recognized the needs of others. He promised to honor Christmas in his heart and to try to keep the spirit the year-round.

May the Spirit of Christmas do as much for all seniors.

• • • •

Cold

> *"And mama in her 'kerchief and I in my cap*
> *Had just settled our brains for a long winter nap."*
> —A Visit from St. Nicholas

As a child I wondered why people wore caps in bed. It was almost as puzzling a question as how Santa Claus got down the chimney. Growing older, this last was easily solved—he didn't. But it is only recently that I have grown to appreciate the rationale for covering the head while sleeping.

For centuries ways were found to live in cold climates without burning non-renewable energy. More recent generations gathered at an open-hearth that radiated good cheer as well as warmth. Copious chimneys whisked away remaining heat as soon as the fire went out. The hazard of fire dictated that all embers be banked or extinguished when families retired. Bundling beneath bed-covers conserved personal heat and kept bodies snugly warm in those frigid bedrooms. But the head protruded because of the need to breath. Above the covers, the head was vulnerable to cold unless covered by thick hair or a cap.

The brain requires a rich and relatively constant flow of warm blood and its circulation is not affected by extreme temperature variations. Thus, cooling the head drains away body heat. Cold constricts blood vessels in the hands and feet to slow heat loss. Restricted circulation increases the blood volume stored in the torso and head. Then our kidneys respond by augmenting the output of urine.

Our generation has been the first and only one to benefit from plentiful and cheap energy. In our life time we have squandered the fossil fuels which took millennia to form. We have become so accustomed to its abundance that national leaders are willing to fight wars to continue America's access to vanishing resources.

Over the centuries, humans adapted to cold in many interesting ways. Eskimos, as an example, have smaller extremities and a 30 percent higher metabolic rate. They eat more fat to support their higher metabolism. More fat is stored in the skin to act as insulation. Fortunately, Eskimos can assimilate fat better than Europeans and they seem to have no problems with cholesterol. They are not long-lived people, however. Perhaps their metabolism "burns" them out sooner.

While resting and relaxed we have a metabolic level that produces about 350 BTUs each hour. Shivering or activity such as walking increases the output to 900 BTUs. Rapid walking up an incline raises the heating rate to 1,200. An athlete competing in a marathon run will exceed 5,000 BTUs per hour. This is equivalent to the output of a bathroom heater. Knowing the great amount of heat we are capable of producing, we begin to appreciate the possibilities and importance of heat conservation. It is possible to live warmly with suitable clothing in an insulated shelter. But it requires sufficient food to supply the fuel.

We "naked apes" (humankind) adjusted to climatic extremes only because we had brains and used them. We invented clothing and devised shelter to create small personal climate areas for survival. Today's high costs, limited incomes and patriotic fervor are inducing some of us to downgrade our shelter. We drastically lower our house temperatures. Yet this may not be wise because deliberate exposure to cold can be perilous. Chilling predisposes to everything from infections and flu to heart attacks and stroke. Cold is a stressing agent. It interferes with body functions. Muscles become stiffened, senses numbed. Increased urine output poses the danger of dehydration Red blood cells cannot give up oxygen when their temperature approaches 20 degrees Celsius (68F). Thus when your hands become so cool, circulation is of little value. Hypothermia and death result when the body's internal temperature drops below 20 degrees Celsius (68F).

The "comfort zone" of 22C (72F) is established as suiting the average adult who is active and dressed. It is not a comfort zone for either the young or the old. For their small size, infants have a disproportionately large skin surface through which they lose heat. The aged who avoid heart attacks because they are not overweight can succumb to cold because they lack insulating fat. All persons beyond the prime of life have significantly less muscle, and they are less active. Muscle action is the principle source of heat that keeps the internal body temperature close to 37 C (98.6 F). Various ailments commonly found in the elderly diminishes their tolerance to cold. These include a general weakness, anemia, thyroid deficiency and rheumatism. A comfort zone for many seniors is probably closer to 26 C (8O F).

If seniors are to survive in colder homes, they must learn to adjust. Although we may have less internal heat available, we can conserve the internal warm climate of our hearts with warm clothing. Clothing is warm when it traps tiny "bubbles" of air within the cloth matrix. The skin warms the air held next to it and once warmed there is no further heat loss. A wind or draft dislodging the warmed air will produce a "chill" factor. That means moving air in a warm room will cool as much as quiet air does at a lower temperature. Dampness will also chill because water conducts heat better than air. It also cools by evaporation. Insulation value is improved when clothing is worn loose and in many layers.

If you must go out in cold weather, wear something on your head. Blood vessels on the scalp do not constrict like those in your hands. A cool head can chill a warm heart. Skip alcohol as well. Its warmth is a dangerous delusion. The warming sensation is only skin flushing that brings your internal heat to the surface where it escapes into the cold air.

• • • •

Heat

A tropical heat wave poses a greater danger to seniors' health than does an arctic cold wave. Heat seems so benign and comforting to us creaking oldsters that its hazard is not apparent. In Tacoma we are prepared for cold but not for heat. After the thermometer rises for a few days, some of us discover that age has tampered with our ability to withstand temperature extremes.

In 1936 I was an intern in Phoenix, Arizona. Summer temperatures regularly soared above 100 degrees Fahrenheit (38 C). Air conditioning was rare, and comfort depended upon the proper architectural construction of buildings. I have two strong recollections of that summer: walking on the grass to avoid the burning pavement and the patients who were overcome by heat. The latter were either young workers, small babies or elderly people.

Workers were brought in straight from the job, usually from the fields or heavy construction sites. They were drenched in sweat, but pale with shock from painful cramps. Sweating had depleted their bodies of salt. The cramps stopped when intravenous saline was given. Further heat cramps could be prevented by taking one gram (1/4 teaspoon) of table salt with each pint of water they drank while at work. When sweating, this excess salt is eliminated through the skin. It does not affect the kidneys nor influence the blood pressure. Baking soda is not a satisfactory replacement because it lacks the chloride which is also lost in sweat.

The elderly were prostrated by heat either in their poorly constructed homes or on the street. Old people don't sweat easily and so they can't gain a cooling effect from sweat evaporation. They become flushed. But flushing is not effective for radiating heat to an environment which is higher than body temperature. Flushing pours a great deal of blood into the skin, which does not return to the general circulation. Circulatory collapse becomes more imminent when there is dehydration, and seniors get out of the habit of drinking water. As blood pressure drops below a functioning level, the person becomes weak, lethargic and disoriented. Rest, cooling the flushed skin and hydration restores the circulation.

Sometimes seniors' circulation is okay, but still,the body temperature rises, just as with a fever. Here flushing and sweating together are ineffective regulators of temperature. Sunstroke may then become an emergency condition. Few recover when body temperature exceeds 108 F (42.2 C). The rising fever causes listlessness. The patient may slip into a coma with possible convulsions and death.

In 1936 we treated sunstroke by plunging the patient into a bath tub of ice water. Vigorous massage assisted the circulation in carrying the cooled blood from the skin to the internal tissues. As the patient's temperature returned to normal, we gave intravenous replacement of water and electrolytes. Afterward, sunstroke victims remain very sensitive to heat.

A heat wave in Tacoma seems unlikely. However, hot weather does hold significant hazards for seniors. Generally Tacoma's humidity is high, so that sweating and cooling through evaporation gives little relief. Atmospheric pollution from automobiles and industry builds up when no rain or breezes clear the air. Temperature inversions retain pollutants close to the ground, where they often reach toxic levels. Seniors with circulatory disease or reduced pulmonary capacity (asthma, emphysema) are the ones most susceptible to atmospheric pollution. Living through an inversion can become precarious when it is complicated by heat. Do remain indoors in cool comfort during the hot hours.

Hot weather is a time to lie about, take frequent cooling baths and drink more. Alcoholic beverages are best avoided, since alcohol causes skin flushing and could augment heat exhaustion. Keep out of the sun. At night open the house for cool, fresh air. In the morning adjust awnings and shades to retain a more livable environment.

• • • •

Jogging

Over the senior scene fads come and go. Now physical fitness looms strong (no pun intended). Daily, more than 20 million adults jog along the nation's byways. Eight thousand joggers will run the Sound to Narrows "Little Marathon." It's a 7.6-mile course through Point Defiance Park and is advertised as a "run for fun" adventure. Many seniors are getting into the social action to enjoy freedom of movement at their own pace. Jogging is not only fun but a part of the treatment program for those who have had a heart attack. At least a dozen patients who had recovered from heart attacks ran in a recent 26-mile Boston Marathon.

The fad has an interesting history. Formerly food had to be wrestled from the land by six days of toil "from sunup to sundown." Humans adapted to this "sweat of the brow" existence. During our lifetime America has gained an overabundance of food, and no hard physical labor was required. Increased leisure did not lessen our appetite nor change our physiological needs. Inactivity now merely brings on degenerative diseases, fat and flabbiness. As we did not adapt to inactivity, we substituted exercise for hard work. In our leisure, spectator sports have become popular and, for only a few, athletics is a profitable career.

In training young athletes, researchers observed that new blood vessels grow to supply increased nourishment for burgeoning muscles. Doctors began to wonder if heart muscles also could gain new blood supplies through physical training. They reasoned that since insufficient circulation causes heart attacks, improved circulation should lessen the danger.

The trick was to gradually increase the work the heart must do. Daily activity is made harder and longer over a period of months. First the heart rate is determined at rest. Then doctors prescribe a mild activity for about five minutes a day. This must be sufficiently vigorous to increase the heart rate by 10 to 20 beats per minute. When the activity no longer increases heart rate, more strenuous exercise is prescribed to again speed up the heart. The duration of the activity must likewise increase up to 15 or 30 minutes daily. Prolongation and repetition of action is the trick to regaining strength and stamina.

A word of caution, however. Seniors with tired old hearts must be careful not to engage in any activity, however briefly, which might race their hearts to more than twice its normal rate. Until you are ready for a Marathon run, you had better keep your heart rate below 150.

A Gallup poll indicated that about 45 percent of surveyed adults engage in some form of regular physical activity. Statistics also show a downward trend in deaths from heart attack. During the decade of the 70s Americans reduced the deaths from heart attack by 30 percent. Who would have guessed that the fad for physical fitness would have so greatly altered the health of a nation in so short a time? Something has caused this improvement in American health. It's impossible to say that the physical fitness fad has not been the reason. Run for your life.

. . . .

Walking

This generation's physical fitness has been sabotaged by television watching and the convenience of the automobile. Rising costs and the infirmities of age are removing the car from the life of many seniors. We are able to preserve our independence only by walking and riding the bus. Our personal freedom started with our first toddling steps out of our mother's arms. Freedom will be impaired when our tottering steps are no longer able to carry us up that bottom step of the bus.

Walking is becoming a forgotten skill that can only be preserved by walking. Disabilities such as those resulting from a stroke can be helped through specific routines suggested by a physical therapist. Then get out and walk. Where? It doesn't matter. I prefer walking along nature paths. There, I can observe the beauty of the Pacific Northwest wilderness and the changing countryside. You may be limited to city streets. Are you afraid of dogs, or of being mugged? Then go with a stout "companion." I don't mean a cane. Canes are for the blind, and for the crippled who depend upon them for physical support. Walking sticks are longer and related to the staff and shepherd's crook. They have been used by common folk since ancient times.

The great advantage of a walking stick is that it imposes an erect posture because it is gripped at shoulder height. One then looks up and ahead rather than at the cracks in the pavement. Margaret Mead used a "thumb stick." Her walking stick was topped with a natural crotch where she rested her thumb.

Walking has the advantage over jogging in that it is more leisurely. You are not left breathless, so you can converse with other walkers, or even stop to chat with a neighbor. You will gain a more intimate knowledge and appreciation of surroundings than is possible with rapid passage. Henry Thoreau could not have made his observations and refined his philosophy had he been jogging around Walden Pond.

Walking can be as strenuous as you wish to make it. If you need to improve muscular tone and heart rate, choose a faster pace over steeper terrain. Ambulating up Tacoma's 11th Street hill will give most of us all the cardiac, circulatory and pulmonary exercise we can handle. That is one place I prefer to ride the bus.

• • • •

Smoking

> *"A custom loathsome to the eye, hateful to the nose, harmful to the brain and dangerous to the lungs"*
>
> —King James I of England

King James was the king who authorized the English translation of the Bible. His 1604 opinion on smoking did not have the scientific background of our Surgeon General's warning of 1964. It was equally ignored by tobacco users.

Smoking is a drug addiction causing cancer, lung and cardiovascular disease and many accidental conflagrations. The annual death toll is more than 300,000: as many deaths as caused by all the violent crimes in this country in the past five years and the 50,000-plus Americans lost in Vietnam.

Incomplete combustion produces smoke. When a fire is hot, combustion is complete and there is no smoke. But cigarettes, cigars and pipes are designed to smolder. Slowly burning tobacco leaf, together with additives, curing agents, fillers and wrapper, releases over a thousand chemical compounds that are contained in the smoke. Only the tar and nicotine content are measured. Yet other chemicals have significant physiological effects. Nitrogen oxide is the same irritating substance found in auto exhaust producing smog. Cyanide and carbon monoxide impair tissue oxygenation and promote cardiovascular disease. Nitrosamines and tar are carcinogens. Even in reduced amounts their presence enhances the cancer causing effect of other substances found in our environment.

Formaldehyde is an irritant that impairs and destroys cilia. Cilia are the microscopic, hair-like structures lining the air passages. Their beating sweeps away particles, keeping the surfaces clean. Removing carcinogens and foreign material is important for preservation of healthy lungs. Chronic cough and excess mucus occur when cilia are no longer there to protect lungs.

A correlation between cigarette smoking and lung cancer is well recognized. But in France, which has the highest per capita cigarette consumption in the world, lung cancer is uncommon. The French do not inhale. French cigarettes, like cigar and pipe tobacco, are made from a dark variety and produces an alkaline smoke. The nicotine of alkaline smoke is absorbed by the membranes of the nose, mouth and throat. In contrast, the acidic smoke of American cigarettes must be taken into the lungs for absorption. This points to the reason people smoke: they seek an effect from the drug, nicotine. Americans inhale to raise their nicotine blood level. Avoiding inhalation by switching to a cigar or pipe will not completely eliminate cancer. Alkaline smokers get their cancers on the lips, tongue, mouth and esophagus.

People try to minimize smoking hazards by using products with low tar and nicotine. Filters reduce the amount of harmful substance in smoke.

To King James' list must be added smoking's affect on circulation and high blood pressure. Smoking causes blood vessel spasm. A single cigarette will lower the temperature in the skin of the fingers and toes. Smokers sometimes develop Renaud's Disease where vasospasm leads to gangrene of the extremities. In addition to this nicotine effect, the cyanide, monoxide and tar products in smoke causes injury to the lining of blood vessels. This leads to arteriosclerosis, heart attacks and stroke. There is still hope, however, for seniors who stop smoking. A year of abstinence will enable the elderly smoker to achieve the same lower mortality rate of the occasional smoker.

• • • •

Habits

The New Year is falsely portrayed as an infant wearing a diaper. Supposedly, it is innocent and fresh. Hopefully it will make proper choices from a world of opportunities which lie ahead. But each year is only an extension of present time and thus can make no choices.

Seniors arrive at retirement like a ship sailing out of a foggy past. We are laden with a cargo of experiences. We also carry barnacles of habits accumulated during our many years at sea. Some of us cast our anchor in the quiet harbor of retirement with relief. Others have been so accustomed to a heaving deck that they stagger and feel useless upon the level ground. It is difficult to break old habits but it can be done. As the diapered child knows, walking is a learning experience. Ambulation requires no further thought when the proper sequence of muscle movements become habitual. The mind is freed for new learning. Too often old habits cling like barnacles to prevent easy adoption of new ways.

The New Year and retirement is a time to change old habits for new, healthier ones. But there is such a plethora of alternatives. Each claims to be the way to greater vitality and longer life. Do we follow the Pritikin, the Mayo or the Beverly Hills reducing diet? Or should it be vegetarian, high protein or high fiber? Maybe we need special food, like yogurt, wheat germ, rose hips or herbal tea. Should we join a health club, take up jogging, weight lifting or dance therapy? We are like a child clutching a dime in a candy store. The range of selection is so great and the unknown flavors so varied, we stand grasping the old familiar ways and do nothing. If you find yourself in this grip of holistic paralysis, dare to take the first small step toward better health. Even a small improvement in lifestyle is better than continuing a detrimental condition by inaction.

• • • •

Will Power

When one arrives at the "golden" years, there is the sudden discovery that a lot of excess baggage has been brought along in the form of bad habits. (The Latin word for baggage is impedimenta.) Our impediments, so easily and thoughtlessly acquired in the days of our youth, now weigh us down like a millstone about our necks. We have reached the time when "coffin nails" are being driven home. It's time to "pay the piper." Your health and life could be at stake.

Now the doctor makes his pronouncement: we have to change, give up those bad habits which have become impediments to good health. Is 60 too late to do any good? No! You will never be 16 again, but failing health will be slowed and illness improved by changing to healthy habits. Changes in eating will lower cholesterol. Losing weight will lessen the load on the heart. Giving up salt will lower blood pressure. Elimination of cigarettes will slow the process of emphysema. Abstinence will allow cirrhosis to heal.

Perhaps you think you haven't the will power. It is not something we are born with, but it is developed through repetitive practice. Will power is a learned skill, and even old dogs can learn new tricks.

Restoring power to the person is done by consciously deciding between alternative choices— yes or no, do or don't, now or later, larger or smaller.

This requires an effort to change actions established over the years as thoughtless habits.

Do you remember the story of Ulysses? His
ship was to pass the island where Sirens sang songs
which caused men to cast themselves into the sea
and die. Feeling that the temptation to join the
Sirens might be too great, he had himself bound to
the ship's mast so that he could not respond. Think
ahead like Ulysses. Then use customs and environmental factors to limit your alternatives. People
don't smoke in church or the elevator. People don't
eat in the library or drink on the bus. Accept personal responsibility for your own health care. Uti-
lize environmental factors that will lessen the temptation to go back to those old and dreadful habits.

The growth of will power is a learning experience accomplished by changing habits. So make a
contract with yourself to achieve whatever goal you
wish. Write it out and then also write down the
obstacles that stand in the way.

Success with a self management program
requires C-A-R-E, as follows:

C ommitment. Without motivation there will
be no success. Set short-term goals, then live one
day at a time.

A wareness. You must understand your
problem and be conscious of old ways.

R estructure the environment so that it will
help you achieve your goal.

E valuate the consequences of whatever
changes you make and evaluate your personal stan-

dards.

Striving for perfection will be self-defeating and probably impossible.

Focusing on environmental and habit changes will assure permanent health improvement.

4 UNDERSTANDING NUTRITION

Food

For a good healthy life, every aspect of food is important to us Seniors. Fresh insights into the cost of civilization come from a recent study of human activity in obtaining food. The study calculated physical work in terms of calories expended each hour by every individual engaged in obtaining and preparing food. The amount of food produced was also expressed in caloric terms. Thus anthropologists were able to measure the efficiency of food production methods and to make comparisons.

Primitive societies, for example, had to hunt for food and could only gather whatever nature provided. Each calorie of effort expended returned about ten calories of food. This was a satisfactory "return on the investment" for laboring less than two hours a day per individual. But there was little opportunity for increasing the amount of food. Adding more workers or working longer hours depleted the supply of food available in the natural surroundings. Primitive hunters and gatherers had to live in a "steady-state" economy.

Primitive horticultural societies, tilled the ground to increase the yield to 11 calories of food for each calorie of work. More people working more hours could increase the total amount of food produced. With the ability to store surplus crops and the use of irrigation, civilization became possible. Close living, land ownership problems and defense of territory made government necessary. A bureaucratic governing elite produces no food but must eat. It siphons off economic growth generated by agricultural laborers. To those workers, the distribution of wealth from the land seems unfair. It is the root cause of present day agitation for land reform in developing countries like El Salvador.

Pastoral societies have an extra step in the food chain: the animals must be fed some of the food. So the caloric yield is reduced to only six for one. However, there is great benefit from always having the food supply readily available.

Improved farming methods, new, more nutritious crops, and selective breeding of livestock have substantially increased the yield of modern agriculture. To the farmer in the American midwest there is a return of over 6,000 calories for each calorie of work by farm workers. An enormous amount of human labor done away from the farm goes into farm production. The work done by tractors, combines, trucks, pesticides, fertilizer and fossil fuels must all be added to the production side of our caloric equation. Modern farming requires more work calories than it returns as edible food calories. For example, each calorie in a can of corn takes ten calories to produce. Every calorie in a beef steak requires 80. Maybe supermarket prices are not out of line.

Before modern agriculture, a peasant farmer could grow sufficient food for his personal consumption by working only 122 hours each year. By contrast, the average U. S. blue collar worker must work over 180 hours annually to earn enough money to purchase his food supply. Does working longer to earn less seem like progress? Perhaps some of us should go back to raising a portion of our own food. A personal expenditure of energy in our gardens will return tenfold in flavorful calories. We will also be rewarded in improved health from our outdoor activity. Small really is beautiful—and it conserves energy.

Food is related to well-being and good health. Two of our national holidays center upon food. Thanksgiving was initiated as a day to give thanks for abundant harvest and sufficient food. Christmas, by contrast, is a day which accents the pleasures of eating and drinking. We send holiday goodies as gifts and we're pleased to receive them. We thus associate happiness with a stomach full of candy, cake, cookies and rich flavorful food and drink without realizing that immoderate use can initiate disease and ill health. Obesity, heart disease, hypertension, diabetes, arthritis and digestive problems are frequently precipitated at this time of year by our gustatory over-indulgence. Our ability to consume has its limits. Do enjoy the goodies in moderation!

Moderation is also the watchword when it comes to food additives. No additive, vitamin or trace element is a single key to good health. Each may be critically important when it is lacking. Each can be toxic if taken in an amount beyond that needed for daily requirement. Recently nutrition enthusiasts have overstressed the importance of zinc.

Zinc is an essential trace element. Over 80 enzymes in our bodies contain zinc. However, there are only a few atoms of zinc combined with hundreds of atoms of other elements in each molecule of enzyme. It is needed only in microscopic amounts. Enzymes are used to digest food and to accelerate chemical transformation. Enzymes play a part in nerve conduction, muscular contraction and protein synthesis. Diminished enzyme activity from zinc deprivation will produce a variety of symptoms. Basically, these are loss of appetite, general weakness, impaired growth, slow wound healing and lower metabolism. Zinc deficiency sometimes accompanies acute and chronic infections, alcoholism and liver disease. It has never been shown that these diseases are caused solely or initially by lack of zinc.

Zinc is widely distributed throughout the body in varying amounts. It is highest in bone, muscle, blood, eye, pancreas and prostate. It is believed zinc levels are lower in other organs because enzymes are rapidly formed and secreted rather than stored. Storage of zinc in bone and muscle is not easily removed for daily use. So one must get a daily small supply from food.

Blood of leukemia victims is low in zinc. Nutrition enthusiasts have claimed high zinc intake might protect against leukemia. Other experts believe accelerated enzyme activity from rapid growth of leukemia cells depletes blood zinc. Low zinc has been wrongly linked to diabetes and impotence. The normal active pancreas or prostate produces and secretes large quantities of enzyme. The enzyme and its production is regulated by many factors other than the tiny quantity of zinc needed for the enzyme.

Zinc is very widespread in nature; trace amounts are found in most foods. It is more abundant in meat, eggs, milk and shellfish. Most vegetables, legumes, seeds and grains contain respectable amounts. Even strict vegetarians are able to get sufficient zinc and remain healthy. Children have the greatest need for zinc because they grow rapidly. When they have zinc deficiency it is usually accompanied by serious health problems due to lack of other essential nutrients. Zinc deficiency is practically unknown among people who get enough to eat. Seniors who eat a variety of foods will get all the zinc they need without resorting to food supplements.

• • • •

Diet

Dear Aunt Abby:

Your doctor is right. You could have a heart attack when your blood pressure and cholesterol level get too high. Your being overweight is an additional risk factor. Your plight is a common one among older Americans. We are over-nourished because we like rich food and eat it to excess.

In addition to medication, your doctor has given you a low cholesterol, low calorie diet. If you follow the pattern of most patients, in a short time you will feel better and then begin to fudge on the diet. Probably you will have lost a little weight, the cholesterol might be down a few points and your blood pressure won't be any higher. While the progression of the disease will have been checked, you will never be cured. You will have to constantly struggle with your diet to maintain better health for as long as you live.

Nathan Pritikin is a scientist, not a doctor. He studied populations that did not eat meat or refined sugars. Among these people he found no high blood pressure, no high cholesterol counts, and no heart attacks. His research demonstrated that overindulged and overweight Americans with advanced atherosclerosis (hardening of the arteries) can reverse the disease process. After achieving ideal weight, their cholesterol and blood pressure returned to normal and the diseased arteries widened to provide better blood flow to the heart. The

Pritikin dietary approach to health eliminates all fats, oils, seeds, nuts and sugars, including honey. Meat is limited to 24 ounces a week and preferably in the form of fish or poultry. Eggs are restricted to seven egg whites a week. Only 8 ounces skim milk and 2 ounces of skim milk cottage cheese or yogurt are the daily allowance for dairy products. Fruits, because of their sugar, are also limited in amount.

Now for the good news. He permits unlimited consumption of beans (except soy), peas and vegetables. Also, unlimited quantities of cereal and bakery products with a slight proviso. They must be from whole grain cereals with no added amounts of fats, sugar or egg yolk. One can forget counting calories because these foods are filling, slow digesting and low in calories. People following the Pritikin program get no extra vitamins or minerals. Salt coffee, tea, cocoa, alcohol and tobacco are restricted.

You may feel that your diet, as recommended by the American Heart Association, is pretty limited. Still, it allows three times the amount of meat and fat permitted by the Pritikin diet. Many doctors think Pritikin goes too far, but they do agree he is headed in the right direction to promote better health. Patients who are sufficiently motivated to give up the good life find ample reward in restored health, renewed vigor and a reawakening of over satiated senses.

Good luck in your new life experiences.

Your loving nephew

• • • •

Cholesterol and Bile

The composition of gall stones was first chemically analyzed in 1902. The stones were discovered to have a complex nucleus of 17-carbon atoms arranged in four interlocking rings. Chemists gave the substance a Greek name, cholesterol. Quite logically "chole" refers to bile and "sterol" means stone. After cholesterol was identified in gall stones, the identical four ring 17 carbon nucleus was discovered in many other substances. They thus formed a class, and it was necessary to coin a new name.

The class name "steroid" means "like cholesterol" but people continue to call them by the unsuitable gall stone name. Steroids are found in plants, yeast, molds and fungi. They are also the principal covering of nerve tissue. Hormones and vitamins are also steroids.

Cholesterol in liquid bile is an emulsifying agent. It helps oil mix with water. The fats and oils we eat is first digested, then emulsified with bile and absorbed into the blood stream as fatty acids. When not used immediately for energy, these fatty acids are stored as fat for future use. This frees the bile cholesterol, which is then returned to the liver to be re-secreted as bile.

Since we only need bile when we eat fats, it

is stored and concentrated in the gall bladder. It is at this point that about 20 million Americans begin to have trouble. If a low-grade infection is present in the gall bladder or the bladder does not empty well, the cholesterol becomes too concentrated. It then solidifies, becoming a gall stone.

The formation of stones is more likely to occur when blood cholesterol is high. Because women "normally" have higher cholesterol levels than men, they also have more gall stones. In medical parlance there is an aphorism called the "4 F's." It states that stomach pain in a female who is fair, fat and forty, is likely to be caused by gall stones. But this aphorism is not always reliable. Among the Navajo Indians it is the dark, thin old male who is more subject to gall stones. I don't know why this is so, but all seniors beware—and keep that cholesterol level low.

A diet that is low in cholesterol and that uses polyunsaturated fats will decrease blood cholesterol by 10 to 15 percent. Saturated fats are the hard fats from animal sources, while polyunsaturated fats are oils from vegetable sources. When an oil is "hydrogenated," as in hardened peanut butter, it becomes a saturated fat and its cholesterol reducing ability is lessened. Fiber and bran will also lower cholesterol by carrying some of it away with intestinal waste.

Cholesterol is the basic substance which organs use to manufacture hormones. The pituitary gland in the brain secretes a host of steroid hormones which regulate other endocrine glands producing additional steroid hormones to govern growth, sex changes and many other body functions.

Dihydrocholesterol is contained in the fatty layer of the skin. When skin is exposed to sunlight, ultra-violet radiation changes the cholesterol to vitamin D. This vitamin is essential for the calcification of bones. The absence of vitamin D in the skin, or in the diet, causes the soft bones of rickets. Another steroid is digitalis, a heart medicine made from the green leaves of the fox glove plant.

With steroids so widespread in nature and making such important contributions to life, why should we avoid cholesterol in our food? The answer is that we usually get too much. Excess cholesterol accumulates within the layers of arteries. and becomes the hardening substance found in arteriosclerosis. When vascular linings are swollen with cholesterol, the inside of the vessel narrows. At that point, a greater force is needed to push blood through the arteries. High blood pressure develops. In time, cholesterol deposits may so restrict blood flow that little will get through. Cholesterol deposits also weaken the arterial walls. In this weakened state the walls can rupture, resulting in hemorrhages. All this is simply to say that too much cholesterol can cause heart attacks and strokes.

One might question the cholesterol-reducing value of polyunsaturated oils like corn oil. Doesn't a farmer fatten his pigs on corn to make that cholesterol-loaded bacon? Of course, but corn also is loaded with starch and sugar — and the farmer helps. Wild pigs are lean and never get as fat as domestic hogs. The farmer starts out with proper breeding stock, the kind that is more efficient in converting calories into fat. Then he puts plenty of food in the trough. The pig, for its part, eats everything put before it. Finally, the farmer keeps the pig in a pen so that he can't run about and get exercise.

Now if you don't want your body to make huge quantities of cholesterol like the pig, you must have a lifestyle different from that of the pig. If it were possible, a person should select slim parents, because genes play an important part in both our chemical and biological makeup. But since we don't have that choice, we must make do with what we have. Make the extra effort to step away from the dinner table. All we eat above our basal requirements turns into fat and more cholesterol. Finally, get into the habit of regular exercise. Physical activity will burn up much of the fat and unneeded cholesterol you consume.

· · · ·

Cholesterol and Colon Cancer

It was a mystery worthy of Sherlock Holmes.* Why should carcinoma of the colon be a

---

* Sherlock Holmes is a fictional character. His inventor, Sir Arthur Conan Doyle, M.D., patterned Holmes after Dr. Joseph Bell, a diagnostician.

common cancer in America while it is rarely found in Africans? Extensive investigation has turned up many clues. Now we think the "villain" has been discovered. Research first led to suspecting that Americans had a genetic susceptibility to cancer because of the obvious racial differences. Then that hypothesis was disproved by epidemiologists studying the Japanese in Hawaii. In Japan, as in Africa, colon cancer is infrequent. But the Japanese who migrated to Hawaii have cancer just as often as other Americans in that state. This focused attention upon diet changes.

The most obvious dietary difference was the fiber content. Americans, with a diet consisting largely of refined foods, get only one-third of the fiber found in the foods eaten by people in the rest of the world. Fiber alters bowel function by increasing stool volume and frequency. Could constipation alone cause cancer? Researchers did animal experiments with carcinogens which showed that there was no direct relationship between cancer and the use or avoidance of fiber. Carcinogens are substances which induce cancer changes in living cells by contact with them. A second difference in the American diet is our great consumption of meat and animal fats. Further study of the Hawaiian-Japanese showed that the frequency of colon cancer correlated to their adoption of American ways and eating habits. Although Americans have helped to shoot McDonald's hamburger count into the stratosphere, they have also suffered 100,000 colon cancer cases each year for their effort.

But how does meat cause cancer? Chemists have shown that cholesterol in animal fat will form a carcinogen when it is subjected to high heat, as when it is broiled. Bacteriologists have also shown that anaerobic bacteria living in the large bowel will do the same thing. These bacteria are adept at converting any cholesterol reaching the colon into carcinogenic metabolites.

Now that we have all the clues, let's line up the suspects and re-enact the crime. The villain is our old enemy, cholesterol.

Americans, with their meats and other fatty animal foods, eat an excessive amount of cholesterol. The surplus, together with secreted bile cholesterol, ends up in the bowel where bacteria turns it into carcinogens. Prolonged contact with colon cells makes them cancerous. Diet fiber can be a helpful and protective substance. Fiber's inert bulk will dilute and combine with cholesterol. Its laxative action shortens the time that harmful carcinogens can remain in contact with living cells.

•　•　•　•

Cholesterol and Lipoprotein

There was a fat lady from Kent
whose diet ideas were well meant
But her clothes got so small
they didn't fit her at all
And now she is wearing a tent.
— Smitty, "Bard of the Rock"
Bainbridge Island

Cholesterol is a waxy substance that is insoluble in water. It is present in all animal fats, including fat ladies. It causes arteriosclerosis by hardening and plugging the arteries. Researchers have recently discovered how this waxy material travels through the watery blood to become lodged in the arterial walls.

Cholesterol is soluble when it combines with another substance called lipoprotein. These are associated with edible fats and oils. Low density lipoproteins (LDL) are larger and carry more cholesterol than the smaller high density lipoproteins (HDL). But LDL has the disadvantage that when it gets inside certain cells it is destroyed. Thus it dumps its load of cholesterol within the cell. HDL, on the other hand, goes in and out of cells picking up the excess cholesterol the cells are not using. HDL transports cholesterol to the liver where it is excreted in the bile. High density lipoproteins seem also to produce more liver and gall stones. (Cholesterol, in fact, literally means liver stone.)

This two-way transport works well when total cholesterol is not too high. Some people with high cholesterol seem protected against arteriosclerosis. They have a high HDL ratio. Women are blessed with a normally higher HDL than men. Any individual can raise his HDL level by physical activity or by the moderate use of alcohol

Some doctors test for HDL in their patients. Others feel that this is a waste of laboratory time and patient's money. The total amount of cholesterol is the critical factor. Good health results when total cholesterol is reduced.

Changing the LDL to HDL may initiate other problems. In two fully matched studies, lowering the HDL ratio decreased cardiovascular deaths but did not improve the overall mortality rate. For some reason, more of the test people died of cancer than in the control population.

Activity and diet are the best means we have for lowering cholesterol. To begin, substitute vegetable oil for animal fats, and margarine for butter. Avoid eggs and whole milk. Eating less calories so that one loses weight will reduce the blood cholesterol. Bran and fiber in the diet also help by tieing up cholesterol in the intestinal tract. Meat itself contains the same percentage of cholesterol as the fat that the butcher has cut away. Perhaps a vegetarian diet might have helped the fat lady from Kent remain a bit more stylish.

· · · ·

Vitamins

For countless centuries there have been mysterious diseases that raged along with every war and famine. They also appeared during long sea voyages. In 1753 James Lind, a naval surgeon, associated one mystery disease with diet. Scurvy disappeared from the British navy following the regular use of citrus fruit. And that is how the English sailor acquired the sobriquet of "limey."

By 1911 most of the other mysterious diseases were known to be caused by a lack of specific substances usually present in food. When these substances were isolated they were found to be vital for normal growth and health. These vital factors seemed to be in a class of chemicals called amines. So a name was coined "vitamine" — with an "e" at the end. When other vitamins were found that were not amines the "e" was dropped and the pronunciation modified. But their vital importance to good health remains.

One would postulate that those ancient mystery diseases would now be found only in the history books. Not so. Vitamin deficiency diseases still smolder among the elderly. Too many live alone and dine on convenience foods. From the sameness of their daily fare, one might conclude they were on a 16th century sea voyage far from the bountiful harvest of shore and supermarket.

Some vitamins are not absorbed and retained in the body for more than a few days. So deficiencies appear whenever the "voyage" is prolonged. Variety is necessary because vitamins are not evenly distributed in all foods. Dietary restrictions or difficulty in digesting and absorbing food can lead to deficiency. A food's natural vitamin content can also be destroyed by storage, processing and cooking. Food processors sometimes replace some of the principle vitamins but they hardly duplicate the spectrum found in nature. Fresh natural foods prepared with minimal cooking are best.

Drugs can interfere with and destroy vitamins. The most common are oral antibiotics, oral steroids and alcohol. Usually when such drugs are taken, extra vitamins are needed. Mineral oil laxative will carry off fat-soluble vitamins but these are stored and less critical unless oil is taken daily.

All cells suffer when there is vitamin deficiency but those covering body surfaces are the first to give warning. Be suspicious of all sores on the skin, mucus membranes and eye surfaces. There may be itching, chapping, cracking and even bleeding. Often vitamin depletion causes soreness in the mouth and gums as well as poor appetite and general fatigue. Diarrhea will accelerate the progression making it more difficult to eat and absorb a proper diet. Better not let it get that far along by eating a variety of fresh foods and popping a vitamin pill now and then.

The Pilgrims came to these shores to escape persecution and to find political and religious freedom. They also expected to find opportunities for increasing their fortunes. Instead they found an opportunity to starve. It is little wonder that the festival of Thanksgiving that second fall was a celebration of sufficient food.

America has continued to produce abundant food and many of us have become corpulent through over indulgence. Inhabitants in other parts of the world are not so fortunate. They live with malnutrition and periodic famine. Most of third world arable land is used to grow export crops: bananas, coffee, cotton and beef. In Honduras, the poorest Central American country, 70 percent of the population is rural and 40 percent of rural people live on 20 cents a day. Less than 12 cents of each dollar from banana sales stays in Honduras.

But there is also hunger in our great land of plenty. Inflation and unemployment have created pockets of poverty throughout the nation. Seniors, particularly, find difficulty in stretching meager dollars to cover many desperate needs. Right here in Tacoma, charity food banks provide food to 10,000 people each month. Enough is given away to prepare about 100,000 meals. If my mathematics are correct, that averages out to only one meal for each individual every three days.

Good nutrition depends more on food quality than the quantity of calories consumed. High quality food with variety is costly. Quality foods provide vitamins, minerals and trace elements so essential to good health. Deficiency in trace elements like zinc causes poor healing and decreases immunity to disease. Beef is a complete protein and contains more zinc than poultry, fish or dairy products.

A 1977-78 study of human nutrition by the U.S. Department of Agriculture found that food choices were most important for continued good health. The study analyzed nutritional content of food actually consumed by elderly persons and calculated its retail cost. In general, good nutrition was directly related to greater expenditure for food. Usually one had to spend at least $1.82 daily. Careful shoppers, by using inexpensive cuts of meat, like heart and liver, could obtain a "reasonably nutritious" diet for $1.59. Ten percent of the elderly who lived alone spent less than $1.43. This study is now over 14 years old.

Time and inflation has only increased the number and worsened the condition of the low-income elderly.

• • • •

Constipation

In America, it has been said, sex is the concern of youth, while the middle-aged worry about their children, and the elderly are pre-occupied with their bowels. Americans purchase $200 million worth of laxatives annually. Their constant use assures continuance of the symptoms the laxative is supposed to correct.

Constipation is an indefinite condition recognized by infrequent bowel movements with hard stools. It is generally associated with faulty eating habits, stress and changes in the environment.

One false belief about constipation is that it causes "auto-intoxication." This condition is erroneously held responsible for everything from poor complexion to headaches to sluggishness to a general malaise. Actually, the reverse may be true—a bad disposition can also cause constipation. Emotions, like worry, apprehension, resentment and anger, profoundly affect the stomach and intestinal tract. Well documented are changes in blood supply, motility, spasticity and secretions.

It may be normal to have a bowel movement several times a day or as seldom as once in three days. It depends on diet and habit. The contents of the colon (large bowel) includes unabsorbed food particles, indigestible fibers, bile waste, enzymes, water and micro-organisms. These latter continue breakdown of food and fiber for as long they're kept in the colon. They also produce methane gas. Water is absorbed making the stool ever drier and harder. Like the small intestine, although less efficient, the colon absorbs bile, sugar and salt.

Bowel habits reflect eating habits. A person can live for weeks on highly refined nutrients given intravenously. During such times one would not have, nor need to have, a bowel movement. In like manner, when nutrients similar to the intravenous solution are eaten as food, little waste will remain after they are digested and absorbed.

For better bowel movements, you must eat food with more indigestible bulk and fiber. Corrective foods are fruits, vegetables and whole grain cereals with high fiber residues. Because excessive rough and indigestible material will sometimes cause distress, seniors must use caution when embarking on a high residue diet. It is equally important to drink lots of water.

Benvenuto Cellini, who lived to be 71, reported that in his later years he ate mostly bread, milk and raisins. Milk and raisins haven't changed much since 1562, but bread has. There is nothing quite comparable, not even the over-rated, over-priced bread baked by Continental Baking Co., with its added "vegetable fiber" more commonly known as sawdust.

Long retention of undigested material in the colon poses three dangers:

• Water is removed making the stool too firm and hard. Passing a dried, hard mass may become so difficult that the straining could induce hemorrhoids or a cerebral hemorrhage.

• Long retention because of weak abdominal muscles may result in an impaction . This blockage must be broken up and removed manually. Symptoms of impaction are fullness, cramping and leakage of material around the obstruction.

• The final danger from chronic constipation is cancer of the colon. Infrequent bowel movements will allow carcinogens to remain in contact with bowel tissue for long periods. Carcinogens are produced by bacteria breaking down cholesterol.

Keeping physically active, eating vegetables and whole-grain cereals and drinking an abundance of water will go far toward keeping you regular. On rare occasions a small enema or a soft bulk laxative, like metamucil, psyllium seed or milk of magnesia, can be helpful. Mineral oil should ordinarily be avoided because oil captures and removes the oil-soluble vitamins you need.

• • • •

Laxatives

Laxatives are assumed to be harmless and thus safe for over-the-counter sales to everyone. Besides, they are a lucrative business. The greatest danger in self-medication is postponement of proper diagnosis of a possible underlying disease. Any change in usual bowel habits or stool appearance is a signal that something could be seriously wrong. In the elderly, the repeated or prolonged use of laxatives may pose health hazards.

One should be aware of the wide range of laxatives available and how each works. Although castor oil, for example, was used by the ancient Egyptians, it irritates the bowel and causes cramps. Castor oil also causes excessive secretions and loss of body fluids. Among the elderly, fluid loss can cause dehydration and electrolyte disturbances.

In the past castor oil has been used in prisons as a sadistic form of punishment. Well-meaning mothers once gave the treatment to their children as sort of a spring cleaning of their insides.

Modern, and better tasting laxative tablets have a similar stimulating action, but they are milder than castor oil. Tablets are today the most widely used form of self-treatment for constipation.

Absorption of as much as 15 percent of the active ingredients in a tablet is of some concern. This can produce allergy in the sensitive person. Additionally, some laxatives are toxic to the liver and can even cause jaundice.

Mineral oil works because it is indigestible and stays in the bowel. It will soften hard stools but it prevents the absorption of fat-soluble vitamins. It can seriously interfere with digestion and therefore should never be taken with meals. Nor should it be used in combination with other laxative agents.

Bulk producing laxatives are somewhat similar to mineral oil in that they are indigestible. They absorb water and swell, holding the water inside the bowel. Adequate intake of water is important, especially with these bulk producing laxatives. Bran and fiber are bulk producing laxatives present in foods.

There are some cautions to be heeded in the use of all laxatives. Where there is any stricture or narrowing of the intestines, bulk laxatives can cause obstruction. Some products interact with medications, particularly digitalis and salicylates (aspirin). Check with your doctor or pharmacist to be sure your laxative is safe to take with your medication.

Saline laxatives were first obtained from natural mineral springs. "Spa" is a mineral spring in Belgium that was once frequented by the Romans. Bathing in and drinking its water was believed to be a cure for many ailments. In the 1800s, spa therapy was very fashionable and popular. Crowds flocked to wherever there was a fancy hotel with a mineral spring. Constipation was held responsible for many symptoms ranging from headache and indigestion to lethargy and "tired" blood. Mineral water and the entertainment amenities that sprang up around these spas appealed to health seekers everywhere. Departing guests took with them the spring water or the evaporated salts to continue use at home. Vichy water and Rochelle salt came from French springs. Epsom salt was originally from a spa near London.

Mineral springs and saline laxatives differ in what they contain. The contents vary in the amounts and combinations of sodium, potassium, calcium, magnesium, sulphur, chloride and phosphorus. Their laxative effect is by osmotic pressure of the mineral content holding water in the intestine. Body minerals and nutrients are drawn in to be carried away with the water and waste. Some minerals from the laxative are also absorbed. This exchange can upset a delicate circulatory balance. Saline laxatives always place a greater load on the kidneys. Some may raise high blood pressure higher. They can also precipitate congestive heart failure.

Improved health attributed to a spa visit is probably due to the relaxing change in a pleasant and hopeful environment rather than its laxative effect. "Taking the water" temporarily cured constipation more predictably and less harmfully than "travelers diarrhea." Both, however, induced a clean out.

. . . .

Diabetes

In the first century B.C., a Greek physician described a condition which caused the "flesh and limbs to melt down into urine." Some 600 years later another physician reported a patient with "honey urine." Only in the last century has this strange malady been identified as a deficiency of Insulin. Insulin is produced by special "islet" cells of the pancreas and released directly into the blood system. Insulin is essential for storage and the utilization of glucose (blood sugar). All sugar from food changes to glucose when disgested. When not used or stored, glucose overflows into the urine. Even one's own muscle protein and fat is converted to glucose, and is "melted down into urine."

While less than two percent of the general

population have clinically detectable diabetes, at least 50 percent will show some signs of abnormality in utilizing sugar by the time they're 60. Seventy-seven percent of diabetics are overweight before the onset of the disease. With advancing age, there is even a closer correlation between obesity and diabetes. While we can't stop getting older, we can certainly stop being fat.

The classic diabetic symptoms are excessive urination, thirst, hunger, dry itchy skin, weight loss and weakness. The weakness is often first noticed in going up stairs. Less common, is sudden changes in vision because blood sugar level can affect the eyes. High sugar in the skin and membranes encourages bacteria and yeast growth. This leads to boils, carbuncles and monilial yeast infections.

There can be early arteriosclerosis and vascular degeneration of the small capillaries before diabetes is diagnosed. This causes tingling and aching, especially of the body and feet. It becomes worse at night. Decreased circulation from arteriosclerosis results in leg cramps, cold feet and numbness. Injuries heal slowly and may ulcerate or become gangrenous. Small hemorrhages and degenerative patches can also occur in the retina of the eye. Other nervous system deterioration is evidenced by impotence and loss of the knee-jerk reflex. A low thyroid condition associated with diabetes is also found.When we eat carbohydrates, the food is digested and absorbed as glucose. As digested starch and sugar enter the circulation, blood glucose levels rise. Higher blood sugar triggers release of insulin that puts glucose into body cells for either use or storage. As glucose is removed from the circulatory system, blood sugar returns to normal. In some people the blood sugar continues to drop beyond the normal level, causing hypoglycemia.

The brain uses only glucose as its source of energy. Without sufficient glucose, there is mental confusion and blackout. This is called "a hypoglycemic reaction or insulin shock." At the other extreme, too much glucose is like putting too much fuel on a fire—the fire gets smokey instead of burning brightly. Just so, diabetics with high blood sugar produces partly burned glucose called ketones. Ketones are acidic and toxic to the brain. Diabetic coma is the the result of too many ketones in the body. Diabetics must walk this tight-rope all day with every meal for the rest of their lives.

Discovery of a diabetic tendency is made by checking the blood sugar level after eating. To standardize the test a measured amount of glucose is given. Then blood glucose is measured at intervals to see how quickly blood levels return to normal. Blood glucose should never get too high and it should be back to normal in two hours.

Diet is a very important part of diabetic treatment. Essentially, diet depends upon slower digestion of starches, and obtaining glucose from protein and fat sources. When blood glucose increases slowly after eating, less insulin is required.

Many Seniors precipitate the onset of their diabetes by overindulgence in holiday fare and sweets. Many overweight diabetics can regain their ability to handle carbohydrates by reducing their weight to normal.

The 1940 census showed Rhode Island and Arizona had the same number of people, yet, in Rhode Island there were three times as many diabetics. E.P. Joslin, the leading American authority on diabetes, came to Arizona to find out why. Race was thought to be a factor because Indians were a significant segment of the population and they weren't supposed to have diabetes.

Joslin's tested samples of the Indian population to find they were just as susceptible to diabetes as Europeans. Perhaps since Arizona was such a young state with a younger population, doctors there had not looked for diabetes nor reported it. After the age difference in state population was adjusted, the incidence of diabetes in Arizona was equal to that of Rhode Island. Dr. Joslin reported that his Indian diabetics were all overweight and their favorite food was peaches canned in heavy syrup.

5 UNDERSTANDING CIRCULATION

Anemia

Blood has always been recognized as essential to life. Animals and people died whenever they lost too much. The Biblical Hebrews believed blood contained an animal spirit of life given by God. Blood as spirit was holy and sacred. The kosher preparation of food requires that animals be drained of blood so that blood is not eaten. Hunters and butchers also drain blood from freshly killed animals because the meat keeps better.

There was a time when Doctors thought many illnesses were caused by "bad blood." The logical remedy was to get rid of this bad blood by bleeding the patient. This practice probably killed more people than it helped, including the father of our country. George Washington was bled twice during his last illness because he was struggling to breath with a "membranous laryngitis" (diphtheria?). He didn't struggle as much after the bleedings.

Blood is important because it carries oxygen and nourishment to our cells. Wastes are removed as the blood returns to the heart, lungs and kidneys. Red blood cells transport oxygen and exchange it for carbon dioxide. White blood cells are the infection fighters that kill bacteria, remove dead cells, and any foreign material. There are also small bodies called platelets which break up at injury sites to cause clotting and prevent further loss of blood.

These cellular elements are made in the red bone marrow and in the lymphatic tissue. Iron is the prime constituent of hemoglobin and we get iron from meat, eggs, and the green vegetables we eat. In iron deficiency anemia, red blood cells are smaller, very pale, and lower in number. This type of anemia follows loss or destruction of blood. It also is common when diets are inadequate.

Red blood cells last only about 120 days so the bone marrow keeps pretty busy making new ones. There must be a doubling of deoxyribonucleic acid (DNA), the neucleoprotein of chromosomes, for cells to divide. Vitamin B 12 and folic acid are necessary to synthesize DNA. An adequate supply of B 12 is present in meat and many foods, but it isn't absorbed into the blood stream unless an "intrinsic factor" is present. What is this factor? It is found in stomach acid, which many elderly no longer produce. When this happens, a condition called hypochlorhydria occurs. The symptoms of hypochlorhydria are a sore tongue and pernicious anemia. Pernicious anemia is characterized by an insufficient number of red blood cells, but each cell is overfilled with iron-rich hemoglobin. It as sometimes called "hyperchromic anemia."

Unhappily the lack of vitamin B 12 also produces neurologic disturbances, initially noticed as numbness in the hands and feet. Eating raw liver will supply the intrinsic factor needed to absorb B 12, but at this stage B 12 is best given by injection.

After about 120 days in circulation, remnants of worn out red blood cells become bile pigment. When too many red cells are destroyed, one not only becomes pale from anemia, but also may turn yellow with jaundice.

Anemia usually accompanies most chronic illnesses. It is a symptom of reduced body efficiencies. It may also be caused by a change in diet. When the underlying chronic disease is properly treated the patient soon recovers from the anemia. It is when anemia is found in association with malignancy, leukemia, or renal disease that it is particularly serious.

Doctors view anemia as a symptom rather than a disease. Healthy old people are not anemic. But if you do suspect that you are anemic, self-treatment is unwise. Anemia has so many possible causes. Taking iron tonic is not the best answer for "tired blood."

Additionally, if a person should take more iron than is needed, the excess iron can cause hemochromatosis. This in turn leads to liver disease, diabetes, skin discoloration and heart failure. Best to go see your doctor.

.   .   .   .

Blood Loss

> *"Fight on," cried Sir Andrew Barton,*
> *"I am wounded, but not slain.*
> *I will lie me down and bleed awhile,*
> *Then rise up and fight again."*
>   —Ancient Ballad

Sir Andrew had the determined spirit we all admire. We should never let any minor setback deter us from a worthy objective. But as a doctor I would say that Sir Andrew had faulty knowledge of human physiology. His bleeding should have been immediately stanched to assure that he would be able to get up to fight again. It is true that some recovery from blood loss follows rest. A better way is to replace the blood lost with a transfusion. It makes recovery quicker and assures better healing of wounds.

Modern surgeons intentionally produce wounds as deep and grave as any inflicted in ancient battle. Yet they are seldom fatal because of significant differences. Doctors cut more slowly, inspecting each layer as the operation proceeds. Blood vessels are visualized and clamped before they are severed. The open ends are either tied or cauterized so that very little blood escapes.

Whenever much blood is inadvertently lost, it is replaced by transfusion. Generally intravenous fluids are given to prevent or correct the dehydration that often accompanies illness. These procedures maintain a proper circulation, which is most important for recovery.

Our blood volume is about 8 percent of our body weight. These few quarts of blood generally fill only about half of all the blood vessels at any one time. This is satisfactory because seldom is blood needed everywhere in the body at once. So the body just shunts blood from inactive places to organs that need the circulation. After eating, the stomach, intestines and liver require extra blood for digestion. It is obtained by taking some away from inactive muscles. Swimming and other strenuous activities following a meal will shunt blood away from the stomach to the muscles. This means, of course, that digestion will have to wait. (Now you know why Mother told you to wait an hour before swimming.)

Most parts of the body can postpone their need for circulation. An important exception, however, is the brain. It has no shunting mechanism. Within seconds after brain circulation is reduced it stops functioning. I picture Sir Andrew getting clobbered, then looking at his bloody wound and passing out.

Were that the case, Sir Andrew would have triggered a psychosomatic reflex that can be initiated by pain and perception. The reflex causes all blood vessels to relax and open. As vessels fill, there isn't enough blood left over to return to the heart for circulation. Because gravity drains blood away from his head, the fainting knight falls from his horse. Now stretched out on the ground, gravity pours blood back to his brain. Consciousness is restored but he shouldn't stand up or return to the fray until the bleeding has stopped. His blood volume will be slowly restored by plasma from his tissues and whatever liquid he drinks.

· · · ·

Normal Blood Pressure

I thought my grandmother wasn't normal. Her blood pressure was more than 80 points below what I thought it should be. At the time I was only a medical student and was trying out my first blood pressure instrument on the family. I worried that she might have some obscure disease, although she seemed as peppy as ever. When I talked to my professor, he laughed and told me I was confusing terms. The usual or normal pressure of a population was not necessarily normal for a particular individual.

Paramedics and nurses, like medical students, do not have the experienced knowledge of doctors. They cannot state what is "normal" for you individually. This is especially true if you are under treatment. Blood pressure medication is sometimes so effective that blood pressure is lowered below the point needed for proper function of vital organs (brain and kidneys). What your doctor tries to do is to reduce pressure just enough to prevent it from going higher.

Checks between doctor visits assure that you are following his guidance. A 10 percent variation in reading is to be expected. Blood pressure checks have often been the means of discovering problems needing treatment. So don't pass up a chance to get it free.

Life insurance companies use blood pressure readings to predict risk and life expectancy. Persons with high pressure are more likely to have a heart attack, a stroke or kidney disease. By actuarial experience they have found that high blood pressure early in life is associated with a shortened life span.

Researchers correlate elevated pressure with an accelerated aging process. You can actually slow the aging process by lowering your blood pressure. High pressure damages blood vessels, making it more difficult for blood to circulate through them. In turn, the pressure must go higher for enough blood to reach the brains and kidneys. Although lowering the blood pressure by treatment will not reverse vessel changes, lower pressure does slow the disease process and prevents further damage. Thus you will gain more if you begin treatment of your hypertension before there is too much permanent change. Treatment, no matter at what point you start, will result in better health.

Oh yes, I forgot to tell you that my 80-year-old grandmother had a blood pressure under 100.

And she lived to be more than 100. But some people think that isn't normal either.

• • • •

High Blood Pressure

High blood pressure is normal for a giraffe. Pressure is needed to send blood up that long neck to his brain, 18 feet above the ground. When blood pressure is measured at a giraffe's head it is not high, it's normal. One might suppose that a giraffe would then get a stroke when he bends his head down to drink, but he doesn't. Instead his heart slows and the blood pressure lowers temporarily. Humans have the same regulating mechanism to protect the brain when we lie down. Jumping up too quickly sometimes causes dizziness or fainting because circulation is slow to return to the upright head.

Hypertension is the medical term for high blood pressure. The word means overstretched. Sudden overstretching can burst a blood vessel just like a garden hose.

Gradual hypertension begins in the arterioles. These are the small arterial branchings that end in the capillaries. Our blood pressure goes higher when more arterioles constrict and allow less blood to pass through. The effect is similar to what happens when you shut off a garden hose at the nozzle. The hose overstretchs and may burst if it is old and weak.

Usually our bodies are able to adjust to brief episodes of higher pressure. Prolonged (chronic) hypertension produces irreversible damage to our heart, kidneys, brain, and especially to the blood vessels themselves. Overstretched vessel walls become thickened and clog up with cholesterol deposits.

Early hypertension has few symptoms to signal its onset. In time, however, symptoms can become severe and disabling. Proper treatment of hypertension is effective and best when begun early. Lowering blood pressure will reduce the damage and slow its inevitable course. Have your blood pressure checked today! Check it regularly.

· · · ·

Theories and Practice

"Too soon old. Too late smart."
—Folk saying

A blood pressure of 160/90 is regarded as at the upper limits of normal by the World Health Organization. Symptoms are rare at this level. When pressure is below 180/95, some doctors are reluctant to give potent medication since only marginal temporary improvement is achieved—there could also be side effects. It's better to use simple remedies and change other factors.

High blood pressure often begins to build in younger years and is associated with hardened arteries (arteriosclerosis). Researchers differ as to the cause of arteriosclerosis. Much of the current day discussion parallels the classic philosophical question, "which came first, the chicken or the egg?" Does arteriosclerosis cause high blood pressure, or does high blood pressure cause hardened arteries?

One side stresses the role of cholesterol deposited along the arterial walls. Thickened inelastic walls grow narrow. Pressure rises to pass the constriction. The response is hypertension. Cholesterol comes from faulty diet habits of too much fat, too much carbohydrates, and too much salt. These diet habits are begun in childhood and continue on into adult life. Advocates of this theory point out that the progress of arteriosclerosis can usually be halted by rigid diet limitation and exercise.

The other faction contends that hypertensive *episodes* play the major role in causing arteriosclerosis. As an example, they cite the pulmonary artery which carries blood from the right side of the heart to the lungs. It transports the same cholesterol laden blood as does the arteriosclerotic arteries from the left heart. The pulmonary artery never develops arteriosclerosis unless there is also high pulmonary pressure. High blood pressure, this group concludes, comes from living the "American lifestyle."

The American lifestyle is one of emotional stress caused by competition, frustration, anxiety and repressed anger. To add insult to injury, Americans also indulge in health threatening habits which constrict blood vessels, such as smoking, coffee and alcohol consumption. All of these activities temporarily increase blood pressure. These episodes of high pressure, it is theorized, stretch and damage the arterial walls. Then cholesterol is deposited within the arteries, narrowing the injured areas. This vicious cycle proceeds to further injure the artery with more stretching and deposits—accompanied by ever increasing pressure.

Usually it is not until the fifth decade of life that the cycle's progress becomes significant. By then serious hypertension sets in. But it all started more than 20 years before.

Many doctors don't take time to instruct their patients about good and proper health habits. In the doctor's view it is a wasted effort because, as the doctor sees it, the patient does not follow advice anyway—and the few that do, do so only briefly. It is always difficult to change one's ways.

Doctors realize the importance of breaking the vicious cycle of hypertension. But normalization of lifestyle is slower and less dramatic than pills. So doctors just say, "Don't eat so many calories. Cut out sugar and fats. Cut down on salt, smoking and drinking and exercise more. Take these pills and came back next month."

Many patients are able to improve their health with regular exercise, and a change in diet to reduce salt, cholesterol and calories. Gradual lowering of blood pressure can be accomplished by simply changing old habits. This has the added advantage that arteriosclerotic changes are reversed without the side effects from drugs. You are never too old to benefit from smart adjustments to healthy living.

• • • •

The Heart

Have you ever listened to your automatic washer and guessed which cycle it was in? Most of us can tell when the tub is filling and when it is emptying by a difference in sound the water makes. Blood similarly moving through channels in the heart makes different noises.

In examining your heart, the doctor listens for each click, thump, squirt, gurgle, hiss, whistle, peep, creek, squeak, slosh, hum or murmur to guess just how the blood is flowing. It is quite a feat because the pumping heart goes through a complete cycle of filling and emptying within a single second. Because sound is transmitted in the direction of the blood flow, your doctor listens low in the chest to hear sounds of blood entering the heart. Sounds of blood leaving the heart are best heard high up. The heart has two sides, each with an intake and exhaust valve, and both sides work simultaneously. So don't panic when your doctor gets an intense look on his face while examining your heart. He's just trying to sort out the different sounds to associate them with other factors. What he picks up could make those noises significant.

Your heart is a dynamic living organ, responding to overload by changing its size, shape and rhythm. Thumping your chest gives the doctor a gross assessment of its form, even though x ray and ultrasound are more accurate. The electrocardiograph records action currents produced when muscles contract. Voltage correlates with strength and size. Changes in muscle polarity have both direction, voltage and sequence. All those wire connections are needed to get a three-dimensional picture of action currents. The "squiggles" give a moment to moment record of heart activity as seen by any two of the many leads. Heart attacks leave a permanent record because healing produces scar tissue and scar tissue has no electricity.

Your heart is a remarkable organ. It takes less than half a second to circulate three or four ounces of blood that maintain blood pressure and nourish a body over 200 times as large. Generally it rests for an equal or longer period while it fills to get ready for the next beat. Someone has figured out that each day the heart does as much work as would be required to lift 10 tons to a height of six feet.

By the time we are seniors, that fist-sized muscle has pushed those tons to the top of Mt.

Rainier 10 times over. Doctors used to believe that all this work wore the heart out, just as it would a machine. Now we believe just the opposite—that the heart thrives on work. It has a remarkable ability to regenerate and compensate under stress, as long as its capacity is not exceeded. Hearts fail when outside factors interfere, or when valves are damaged to the point that the heart becomes an inefficient pump.

Arteriosclerotic changes can restrict circulation to the heart muscle. Without enough oxygen and nourishment, the heart muscle cramps. This episode is recognized as a "heart attack."

Irregular heart rate in the elderly is usually secondary to hardening of the arteries. Cholesterol and calcium deposits additionally invade the heart lining and thicken its valves. Rough-edged valves may then leak, forcing the heart to pump a greater quantity of blood. Thickening may also constrict the valve openings, thus making it more difficult for blood to flow.

Sometimes the deposits affect the nearby excitatory and conduction system within the heart, producing a condition called heart block. This will produce irregularity from loss of coordination between the heart chambers. Heart failure results when the heart can no longer pump blood efficiently. Ordinary heart failure is not dramatic, sudden nor painful. The heart just falls a little behind in its work. In time, the accumulated load becomes so great that the heart must work at top speed continuously.

The heart pushes against the blood pressure that is always present in the arteries. When blood pressure is high, greater resistance prevents the heart chamber from emptying completely. During its rest period it gains a greater amount of blood than normal. Overfilling stretches the muscular heart, which responds with a more forceful beat. But sometimes it is too tired or too weak to adequately respond. Blood then accumulates in the veins that return blood to the heart. Pressure in the veins increase and causes excess fluid to accumulate in the body's organs and tissues. This passive congestion can seriously interfere with normal functions.

At day's end, increased accumulation of fluid commonly causes swelling of the ankles. After going to bed the fluid migrates from the legs to the lungs. Pulmonary congestion may cause an attack of "cardiac asthma" that awakens the victim in the middle of the night.

Doctors have a number of ways of combating heart failure. The easiest is to reduce the patient's weight and blood pressure. This significantly lessens the work the heart must do, even while we rest. Since salt is retained with fluid to maintain isotonicity, salt restriction is a means of reducing the volume of excess fluid. Diuretics get rid of sodium (salt), which decreases fluid volume. Digitalis and similar medication can slow the heart rate and improves the strength of each contraction.

Narrowed heart valve openings can be freed by operation. A deformed leaky valve can be completely replaced by an artificial one. When the heart runs too slowly or becomes too irregular, a pacemaker can take over the job.

The heart normally circulates more blood by beating faster. This has the disadvantage of using more energy and of shortening the rest period between beats. Speedier heart beats are a normal response to exercise, but the rate should return to normal after a few moments of rest. It is a sign of lessening heart capacity when a rapid rate is prolonged after only slight exertion. If your heart, after years of quiet toil, is now making you aware of it, you should take it to a doctor.

· · · ·

Heart Attack

Have you ever wondered how activity like shoveling snow could bring on a heart attack? While there are a number of contributing factors, the most obvious is that the victim was unaccustomed to such vigorous activity. Seniors who rarely exert themselves to the point of breathing hard, never discover, until too late, that their heart has lost its reserve capacity. Getting up to change channels on the "boob tube" is hardly a conditioning exercise.

A second factor contributing to heart attacks is cold temperature. Cold causes surface vessels to constrict so that body heat can be conserved. The coronary arteries that nourish the heart constrict in a reflex action to the shoveler's cold hands. Then ordinary exertion, coupled with a slower circulation from the cold temperature, triggers the heart attack.

A third factor relates to snow shoveling itself. When lifting and throwing the heavy snow, we hold our breath. This gives our arms the firm foundation of a rigid chest. Incidentally, it also raises the pressure within the chest cavity. High chest pressure prevents   blood from flowing back to the heart and lungs. After pressure is released, too much blood surges in to temporarily overload the heart. Many an old heart just can't take these sudden changes.

We in the Pacific Northwest seldom have to shovel snow. Still, there is a lesson here for all seniors. First, avoid activities that require you to strain, or to hold your breath to lift. Second, keep your heart physically fit. This requires sufficient exertion over a sustained period of 15 to 20 minutes to increase your heart rate. Naturally, this will cause you to breath deeper and harder. Daily sessions are best but cardiac fitness can be maintained by only two to three sessions weekly. Finally warm up and dress warmly for strenuous physical activity.

•   •   •   •

Varicose Veins

When a person is standing, even for a few minutes, pressure within the leg vessels increases at least five times. As you walk, your leg muscles squeeze the veins producing a massaging effect. One-way valves inside the veins cause blood to move upward. Thus, foot and leg movement helps push blood back to the heart, as if pumped.Veins on the surface of the skin are separated from the muscle massage action by a layer of fat. When skin loses its firm resilience, the vein "pump" does not work well and pressure within the vein rises. The higher pressure causes surface veins to enlarge. Indeed they may enlarge so much that the vein valves cannot close the openings. Consequently, blood leaks downward through the skin valves to overload the veins between the muscles. Those veins must then move this additional blood upward all over again.

The National Institutes of Health in Bethesda, Md., estimates that varicose veins affect one out of every two women, but only one of every four men 40 or older. It is a significant health problem for all seniors. But what explains the difference between the genders?

Women are more subject to varicose veins because their legs are fatter. They also wear more constrictive clothing, like garters and girdles. The latter support the abdomen when standing, but girdles also compress the large leg veins when sitting. Pregnancy, with its higher intra-abdominal pressure, often starts the varicose process. Finally, tradition deters women from putting their feet on a desk, or even on a hassock.

Varicose veins are not just unsightly; they can be uncomfortable, producing itching and burning. Chronic congestion of the veins leads to swelling of the legs and feet. A scaly itchy dermatitis may develop and eventually there may be ulceration. Enlarged veins can become inflamed (phlebitis) and clots may form in the stagnant blood of the varicosities. If clots dislodge, they go to the lungs and cause pulmonary thrombosis that is frequently fatal. Phlebitis was the disease that temporarily crippled, and might have killed, former-President Richard M. Nixon.

For people who must stand or sit for long periods, elastic stockings are of considerable benefit. Support hosiery slows the progression of varicose veins and may be adequate treatment for slight cases. If more severe, the veins can be injected or tied off to prevent blood from flowing down toward the foot. Permanent good results cannot be assured, however, unless the varicose vein itself is completely blocked or removed. This is a minor procedure but complex enough that it should be done in a hospital. To "keep smiling" we add, "keep moving those legs."

• • • •

Hemorrhoids

Hemorrhoids are varicose veins in the skin and lining of the anus. The lay term is "pile" from Latin meaning "soft ball." It has the same derivation as pile carpets made with looped threads. Usually, hemorrhoids are soft, rounded, purplish lumps under the skin. They swell with straining and long sitting. Generally, they cause only slight discomfort.

Skin veins in the anal region connect with the veins of the intestinal tract inside the abdomen. Intestinal veins, loaded with absorbed nutrients, carry their blood directly to the liver. This is the "portal circulation." The liver purifies and stores fats and glucose before returning blood to the heart and general circulation. Veins within the abdomen have no valves like the veins of the extremities. As a result, any slowing or increased pressure in the portal circulation will cause increased back-flow through the hemorrhoids. Hemorrhoids are very common.

Whenever there is increased pressure within the abdomen, anal varicose veins swell and enlarge. Pregnancy, obesity, coughing, sneezing, liver disease and tumors all may increase intra-abdominal pressure. Hemorrhoids become extremely painful when clots form. Typically clots occur while straining to have a hard bowel movement. Clotted hemorrhoids can become inflamed, break down, and bleed profusely. These clotted (thrombosed) hemorrhoids may also shrink and heal spontaneously.

A large constipated stool, combined with hemorrhoidal swelling, can tear over stretched skin resulting in painful anal fissures. Hemorrhoidal veins on the intestinal side of the rectum sometimes rupture and bleed bright red blood. These internal hemorrhoids will sometimes prolapse through the anus to protrude annoyingly.

Since ordinary piles are common and most will heal by themselves within 3 to 5 days, home remedies are popular and useful. Pain and itching can be relieved by analgesic pile salve. Warm compresses or sitz baths are comforting and reduce swelling. Moistened toilet tissue should be used to pat, rather than rub, the area. To soften constipated stools, mineral oil and bulk laxatives are helpful.

Contributing factors should always be searched for and corrected because hemorrhoids are only a symptom of increased portal pressure. Cirrhosis, liver diseases as well as cancer and tumors become more common with advanced age. Invariably consider hemorrhoids to be an early unpleasant warning of an eminently more serious possibility. For seniors, piles are always playing "hard ball."

6 SKELETAL CHANGES

Arthritis

> *"What starts on four legs, walks on two legs and ends on three legs?"*
> — Riddle of the mythological Sphinx

Archaeological findings in the bones of pre-historic man are mute evidence that a cane, or staff must have been one of man's early inventions. Certainly present day seniors know how helpful a mobile support can be to their locomotion. Yet , other seniors hesitate to use this help because they think a "three-legged-gait" might mark them as being "old." To reject so useful a tool on this ground is false pride.

Our joints are like the tires of a car—they wear out with increased mileage. They will also give out sooner if they have been weakened by injury or disease. Unlike tires, joints will lose their ability to move if they are not used. The single thing that most restricts the use of our joints is pain. Often pain will keep a joint almost as still as it would be in a cast. Later, when the pain has abated, the joint can again bear its load, but stiffness will make the limb clumsy and less useful. Just imagine a knee that has stiffened in a bent position. Or, how will a woman with a frozen shoulder raise her arm to comb her hair? Such results are preventable by dulling joint pain and continuing joint movement without load bearing.

Strangely enough, most arthritic pain is not inside the joint. It is in the tissues around the joint. Pain here can be relieved by heat. My personal preference is intermittent rather than continuous heat. Some may find that alternating cold with heat is helpful. Gentle massage can further reduce discomfort. Then the joint should be moved through its range to a point where pain occurs. Hold that position for a moment before backing off. Strive to move the joint repeatedly through its full range without any load or weight bearing. When this is done several times daily, it will keep the joint flexible and strengthen muscles that support the joint. Acutely painful joints must be moved passively, that is, by gravity, or have someone else move them for you.

Many medications can relieve arthritic pain. The simplest and most used is aspirin. No buffering agent is needed when aspirin is taken with food. Alka Seltzer is not advised because of its sodium content. Ibuprufen, (Advil, Motrin) is also an anti-inflammatory agent useful in arthritic pain. Most seniors will be able to increase their joint mileage with HAMM—(No beer endorsement intended)—Heat Aspirin, Massage, and Movement.

• • • •

Joints

The 50,000-year-old bones discovered in the Neander River Valley were hailed by evolutionists as those of a "missing link." The skull was obviously human, but the skeleton appeared to be that of an ape. Curving forward, the spine lacked the lordotic backward bend of the human erect posture. Less biased scientists were not looking for "the emperor's new clothes," but contended that Neanderthal man's spine resembled that of many elderly men.

Osteoarthritis is the curse of growing old. Everyone older than 65 will have some demonstrable arthritic changes in their joints. One in 10 of us feel stiffness and/or joint pains almost daily. For about one in 100, movement will be so restricted that hospitalization or custodial care is necessary. Arthritic deformities occur because muscles that flex or close a joint are stronger than the opposing muscles that straighten it. Thus, knees and hips can become bent, and the fingers may become clawed. The back curves forward as in apes — and the Neanderthal man.

The purpose of joints is to allow movement. They are designed to withstand wear (our bone ends are covered by a thin layer of cartilage). Cartilage is nature's "Teflon": tough, elastic and slippery. With constant use, injury and advancing age, cartilage can become soft, brittle and cracked. It regenerates poorly. It is repaired by growth of bone and connective tissue, which does not withstand as much abuse. Such a joint can work about as well as that old fry-pan with the scratched Teflon.

Arthritis poses a difficult dilemma. Continuous use of arthritic joints may result in more damage and increased pain. Rest brings relief and the opportunity for healing. But following rest there is increased stiffness and the pain returns with movement. Continued inactivity leads to weakness and reduced motion. Not used, a joint becomes use*less*. Escape lies in the judicious use of medication to relieve pain and reduce inflammatory reaction. Pain comes from tight muscles and the grinding together of rough joint surfaces. One should not abuse joints by ignoring the warning of pain.

Yet, if joints are to carry us a few more miles and last our remaining years, it will be because of what we do rather than what we take. Arthritic joints must be moved through their full range of movement several times a day. This should be done slowly, gently and without load bearing. If done under water, say, in a swimming pool, the weight of the limb will be supported.

Wear, and the chance of damage, increase with greater loads. The load a joint must bear is probably twice that of the weight it supports. This is understood when one sees how the joint withstands the weight of the object being lifted, as well as the force of the muscles lifting the object. Injured and overused joints are more likely to have cartilage damage and arthritic changes.

Diet is not a causative factor of osteoarthritis although laboratory tests show that a lard enriched diet produces more arthritis in mice. Perhaps this only indicates that more joint damage comes about with the greater burden of being overweight. Excessive calcium should be avoided, but its role in arthritis is only secondary. Often there is too little calcium in bones (osteoporosis), while at the same time there may be too much in the joints.

The Romans knew the value of moist warmth before the time of Christ. Throughout their empire, hot baths were utilized for healing comfort rather than for cleanliness. The natural hot springs they used remain health spas in our time.   So do as the Romans did. Soak those aching joints in hot water.

Specific treatment of osteoarthritis is limited to relieving discomfort. Avoid cold and dress to keep warm. Heat, in any form, applied to local, painful areas will prove comforting. Self medication should be limited to simple analgesic remedies such as aspirin, acetomenophen (Tylenol) or ibuprufen (Advil). Anti-inflammatory agents play a minor role in this degenerative joint disease. They can be very expensive and may have serious side effects.   Be aware, too, that aspirin can irritate the stomach. Buffered and coated aspirin is less irritating but all forms affect blood clotting and can cause bleeding. Large amounts are toxic to the auditory nerve, causing tinnitus and deafness. Acetomenophen causes liver toxicity when used in prolonged and large doses. It is wise to alternate medications and take only the minimum amount needed to keep yourself comfortable.

After a period of rest or inactivity, stretch slowly, like a cat. This will strengthen extensor muscles and straighten joints. Intersperse brief rest periods between short (15 minute) episodes of activity. Avoid using low, soft chairs or beds; getting up and out of them is an unnecessary strain. Avoid lifting or carrying heavy or awkward objects for the same reason. This could mean losing weight if you are getting heavy and awkward. Those who engage in strenuous activity should remember that a baseball pitcher "warms up" before the game and he keeps warm between innings.

•   •   •   •

Osteoporosis

Ever wonder why some oldsters develop "dowager hump?" Yes, men have it too, but it favors the ladies. As we grow older and become less active, our bones lose their calcium. Mineral loss makes bones more transparent to x rays, and weakens them so that they fracture easily. Compressed spinal vertebrae are wedge-shapped, producing a rounded back. In seniors this curvature is commonly caused by osteoporosis.

Generalized osteoporosis occurs whenever a person gets insufficient calcium in their diet. But there is more to it than just drinking more milk. Growth hormone, parathyroid, pituitary, steroids, sex hormones, fluoride, vitamin D, and phosphorus all play major roles in the calcification of bones. Astronauts flying weightless in space also lose calcium. You lose it while you sleep, as does a limb held motionless in a cast. Inactivity results in calcium loss even when you are getting enough calcium.

Osteoporosis is most common in women after menopause and is attributed to hormone imbalance. Many women have lost calcium during pregnancy. They thus bring less dense bones to their senior years. Replacement of female hormones helps osteoporosis, but many women develop cancer from the stimulation of uterine and breast tissue.

Seniors of both sexes must have more than 500 mg. of calcium daily. If you are not getting enough in food and dairy products, take a pill. People who suffer from leg cramps at night are advised to take calcium at bedtime. Keep active. Even in a chair or bed you can move, squirm, bang your feet and wave your arms just like a weightless astronaut.

Taking too much calcium can be harmful, although most excess calcium will not be absorbed. Unneeded calcium absorbed into the system is deposited in arteries, around joints, in muscle attachments and tendons and in scale that forms on teeth. Calcium is also excreted by the liver and kidneys in the form of stones and gravel. So take enough calcium, but don't overdo it.

· · · ·

Gout

Spring is the time to expect the return of birds, flowers and podagra. Podagra is an ancient and aristocratic disease well known to Hippocrates. The Greek name means "foot trap." Over a million Americans with gout can attest to the descriptive accuracy of the Greek title. Uric acid accumulates in their joints, most commonly the big toe. A slight change in local body chemistry produces crystallization of the uric acid. The effect is like putting sand into the joint. White blood cells respond with an acute inflammatory reaction. Overnight pain becomes throbbing and continuous. Any slight touch or movement is excruciating. There seems no way to withdraw a foot caught in this trap.

Carbohydrates and fats contain the elements of carbon and hydrogen. In the body these are of carbon and hydrogen. In the body these are "burned up" with oxygen to release energy and form the harmless waste products of carbon dioxide and water. Proteins contain the additional element of nitrogen. Were nitrogen to be combined with oxygen it would become caustic nitric acid. Instead it is metabolized to form uric acid. This is then harmlessly excreted in the urine. People with gout are unable to get rid of all the uric acid accumulating in their blood. They handle the surplus by stuffing it into the "nooks and crannies" of the body. Unfortunately for them, these spots are the joints, and wherever else cartilage is found. Uric acid can replace and permanently damage cartilage. It will also impair kidney function, cause high blood pressure and produce kidney stones.

The uric acid of protein comes from two sources. Our own body cells break down at a fairly even rate to release uric acid. Breakdown is increased during strenuous physical activity and when fasting. The other source is the food we eat. We must have protein to replace our body cells, but over-indulgence of high protein foods can cause trouble. Even in Hippocrates day, gout was recognized as a disease of heavy meat eaters among the aristocratic and wealthy. Most damaging are the red meats, gravies and glandular organ meats like liver. Goose, duck, turkey and pork are also harmful since fat in these foods interferes with metabolism of uric acid. Legumes and whole grain cereals are additional high producers of uric acid. And there are other dietary considerations.

In 1703, England lowered the import duty on port wine. Coincidental to the greater consumption of wine there was a marked increase in gout. Wine does not contain uric acid but alcohol interferes with metabolism and excretion of uric acid and so can bring on an attack of gout. There is a long list of drugs that can do the same thing. The list includes liver extract, penicillin, laxatives, diuretics, bile salts and insulin. Is it any wonder that subtle springtime changes in our body chemistry can spring that podagra trap?

Modern treatment of gout strives to increase the kidneys' output of uric acid and to decrease the frequency of attacks. It is incumbent upon each of us to abandon our aristocratic American eating ways for the more healthy and less painful fare of commoners.

• • • •

Back Strain

Oh! my aching back! I knew immediately that I was not lifting properly. My feet should have been closer together: they were spread apart. I should have squatted to use strong leg muscles: I was bending over at the waist. The bulky load proved heavier than I had expected, but it was almost raised when the pain struck. By then it was too late to prevent low back strain.

There are many ways to treat low back pain. What should I do? A faith healer convinces that pain is an illusion of perception. "Pain lies in the head" rather than the back. A psychiatrist might probe my subconscious to find hidden resentment against the task I was doing. Perhaps Yogi meditation would be the way to relief. Should I seek the advice of a friendly pharmacist or buy Doan's pills? Voodoo medicine could use rattles and charms to drive away the evil spirit of pain.

All these methods have their loyal adherents. We, accustomed to the western tradition of medicine, doubt their effectiveness. Our doctors attribute pain to derangement of body structure or chemistry. They search for "abnormalities" and then prescribe the "proper" remedy. Thus, a chiropractor would search for a lesion in my spine. My spine would be manipulated and corrected by adjustments. An internist would locate muscle spasm and prescribe a muscle relaxant. An analgesic for pain might help. A generalist could refer me for physical therapy such as microtherm, ultrasound or massage. If I selected an orthopedist, x-ray photographs would be made. Then I might get a back brace, or possibly a hospital admission for continuous traction.

It is strange that a single illness can be treated in so many ways. It is stranger still that a patient can determine his own treatment through selection of his healer. This is because much illness and disability lies in the perceptions of the patient. Belief and trust in the healer and the methods used are important to the cure. Actually, most conditions are subject to natural recovery. Given half a chance, nature will heal. People will attribute their cure to whatever was done during the time nature accomplished the healing miracle. With recurrence, they seek the old remedy in the unfounded belief that it is necessary.

The increased specialization of health practitioners and ever-rising costs have mandated a greater degree of self-care for seniors. They should follow common sense health habits and avoid situations that might prove harmful. They must rely upon the built-in durability and self-healing of the human organism for recovery.

Seniors ought to use a doctor as one does an auto repairman. When a car has had proper maintenance, it only goes to the shop for repairs. For myself, I prescribed rest for my back. When moving about, I kept my back straight so that it could not be hurt further. I sat in a straight-backed chair with a firm seat. (President Kennedy soothed his aching back in the now famous JFK rocker). Later I found a hot shower comforting. No medicine was necessary as quiet and back support gave me sufficient relief.

• • • •

Sciatica

> *"Thou colds ciatica, cripple our senators and make their limbs halt and lamely as their manners."*
>
> — Shakespeare

Our backbone is like a series of hat boxes stacked one atop the other. Behind is a tent-like structure of bone called the neural arch. Our spinal cord runs through the series of "tents" connecting the brain with all parts of the body. Nerves pass outward through the spaces between the neural arches. Between each of the "hat boxes" there is an elastic cushion, an intervertebral disc. This permits movement between the vertebrae.

Intervertebral discs are held in place by a fibrous ring. With advancing years, the discs can degenerate or suffer injury. When one bends over to lift a heavy object, it is estimated that the hydraulic pressure generated within the lowest intervertebral disc is 10 times that of the weight being lifted. But a degenerated disc can rupture while you are tying your shoelace. Any weakening of the fibrous ring allows the softer disc center to be squeezed out like tooth paste from a tube. When the extrusion occurs beneath the neural arch, and 85 percent do occur here, it presses upon nerves. Sciatica is the result.

Simple mechanical pressure on a sensory nerve causes numbness and tingling that seems to come from beyond the point of pressure. We have all experienced this sensation when, after crossing our legs, our foot "went to sleep." Or we bumped an elbow and caused our fingers to tingle. Nerve pressure from a ruptured intervertebral disc is a similar sensation, but much more serious. Additionally, inflammatory reaction following injury may cause pain.

Characteristically, sciatica begins as a catch in the back. Then the pain and numbness migrates into the buttocks and down the back of the leg. The back will often improve, while pain in the hips and legs grow more and more severe. Any sudden movement like sneezing can be very painful. The sciatic victim will develop a limp and a protective twist to one side. Since stretching the sciatic nerve increases pain, bending over or even sitting is often unbearable. Sitting up in bed without bending the knees becomes impossible. Avoidance of nerve-stretching is sometimes carried to the point where walking is done only on tiptoe.

Pressure upon a motor nerve does not produce pain, but it does stop nerve function. Consequently, there will be weakness leading to eventual paralysis in the muscles served. Commonly, these are the muscles which raise the foot and toes. Often one is not aware of progressing weakness until permanent paralysis occurs. Pressure on a motor nerve must be relieved before this can happen.

When there has been only a small extrusion of disc material, conservative treatment for three to four weeks will allow the symptoms of its presence to disappear. Unfortunately, similar symptoms caused by a large disc protrusion may also improve with rest and time. If operative relief of pressure upon the nerves is postponed for too long, it may be too late to restore function to paralyzed muscles. Then you could end up as halt and lame as a Roman Senator. And if you are in pain, who can blame you for forgetting your manners?

• • • •

Bursitis

"What's in a name? A rose by any other name would smell as sweet"

A bursa is a small sac containing fluid. We have many. They are located over bony prominences and reduce the friction between bone and overlying muscle or skin. When injured, a bursa becomes swollen and painful. The condition is called bursitis.

In popular usage, some bursal injuries have received a name which indicates the cause. Thus, crippling bursitis over the bony prominence just below the knee cap is called "housemaid's knee." Housemaid's knee was a common disability resulting from an outmoded way of scrubbing floors. One might suppose that this bursitis problem no longer occurs. People don't have housemaids, and they now use a long-handled mop. But housemaid's knee has become an occupational hazard of senior men. It comes to the retired handyman who lays the new tile in the kitchen. Or to the gardener, accustomed to getting dirt under the fingernails. A kneeling pad is good insurance to prevent housemaid's knee bursitis.

An anatomically comparable bursa is found just below the point of the elbow. Old time miners, working in cramped spaces with hand tools, would bump their elbows and develop "miner's elbow." No one need go into a mine to find cramped work spaces. Miner's elbow can affect the tinkering automobile mechanic or the home-hobbyist putting up a bookshelf.

Miner's elbow is not to be confused with "tennis elbow," however. The latter is a joint strain rather than a bursitis. It will respond to similar medical care. Tennis elbow occurs on the thumb side where the forearm bone meets the upper arm. Strain to this joint is caused by wrist rotation while delivering a backhand tennis stroke. Some seniors may get the disability while playing tennis. Most will get it turning a screwdriver.

Acute mild bursitis will often subside with just rest and application of local heat. Chronic bursitis often requires aspiration of fluid which distends the sac. In some cases there is crystalized material that should be removed. Medication can be injected to reduce the possibility of recurrence.

7 SENSORY CHANGES

Hearing

The joy of singing in the bath comes from listening to the amplified resonance of your own voice in the tight acoustical confines of a bathroom or shower stall. Listening is important. Intelligent mimicry of sounds becomes the basis for speech and human communication. Hearing-impaired children have great difficulty learning to speak. Until recent years, these children were condemned to be both deaf and dumb (mute).

But deafness in the elderly is different. While able to speak, seniors find that auditory disease frequently destroys their hearing. One consequence of hearing loss is the decrease in human contact. That is because individuals who remain unresponsive to important matters are categorized as "dumb." Here, though, the word is used to mean "stupid," and stupid people do not make very good company.

Deafness arises at many points along the complicated path of sound transmission. The outer ear canal may be blocked by accumulated wax which diminishes sound like the mute used to soften a trumpet's tone. Wax lodged against the ear drum will dampen its vibration. Fluid within the middle ear has the same deafening effect as water in the external ear. An ear drum that has been perforated or thickened by disease will not vibrate easily, and thus, soft sounds remain undetected. Air pressure must be the same on the inside as on the outside of the ear drum. Many of us have experienced this temporary deafness during an airplane descent from high altitude.

Presbyacusis, which literally means "old man's hearing," strikes twice as many women as men beyond the age of 50. In many cases, the cause is the fixation of the three tiny bones which transmit sound vibration from the ear drum to the fluid within the inner ear. It is believed that fluoride in drinking water can prevent this cause of deafness by hardening the bones. In any event, it can be treated by operations that "free up" or replace the bones.

Thomas Edison had middle ear deafness as the result of scarlet fever infection as a boy. He was considered unteachable and left school to work as a newsboy on a train. He could hear people on the train since they raised their voices above the train's noise. Almost completely deaf, he invented the phonograph and left the mark of his teeth upon his personal machine. Sound vibrations were conducted by bone around his middle ear to his inner ear. Edison utilized his substantial deafness to advantage throughout his life. Extraneous noise and chatter never disturbed his meditation or deep thought. Edison demanded that his workers report to him personally whenever they made a mistake. By a succession of "huhs" and "louder!, I can't hear you," he had the poor fellows yelling public confessions for all their co-workers to hear. The same mistake was rarely made twice.

The inner ear is a tapered, coiled and fluid-filled tube about one inch long. The coil makes two turns so it has the appearance of a snail shell. From base to apex it is lined with microscopic hair-like cells which grow progressively shorter toward the apex. These hair cells respond to specific frequencies of vibration within the fluid of the inner ear. Each activated hair cell provides electrochemical stimulation to a nerve at its base. Each stimulated auditory nerve fiber then registers as sound in the brain.

An experimental hearing aid electronically separated sound into five frequency bands. The micro-electric output from each band was used to stimulate five points on the auditory nerve spread out on the inner ear coil. Deaf patients, upon using the hearing aid, judged their restored hearing to be almost normal. However, their own voices seemed softer and more distant because sound now had to travel in air to the hearing device before returning to the inner ear.

Auditory nerve hearing loss is common and it has many causes. Childhood diseases (measles and mumps), head injury, tumors, arteriosclerosis, high blood pressure, a variety of drugs and sounds greater than 100 decibels will cause deafness. Jet engines and rock bands easily exceed 130 decibels. Nerve-poisoning medicines include salicylates, aspirin, quinine and some antibiotics. Fortunately, deafness does not follow unless the drugs are used in large doses or over a long period of time.

Hearing aids can make sounds louder so that they are more easily heard. However, when there is a hearing deficit within only a small tone range, the unwanted amplification of all sound becomes most uncomfortable. For this reason, sophisticated hearing aids are now tuned to selectively amplify in the frequency range where you have a deficit. Modern electronics has miniaturized these devices. Tiny hearing aids can even be hidden within the ear canal. President Reagan preserved a youthful image with such a device. But detractors claim he used it to tune out sounds of anguish coming from the poor and the elderly.

• • • •

Deafness

How does it feel to grow deaf? Ludwig von Beethoven gives us one of the best accounts. In 1800, four years after the great composer began to lose his hearing, he wrote: "To give you some idea of my extraordinary deafness, I must tell you that in the theater I am obliged to lean close up against the orchestra in order to understand the actors and when a little way off I hear none of the high notes of the instruments or singers. It is most astonishing that in conversation some people never seem to observe this. Often I can scarcely hear a person if he speaks low; I can distinguish the tones but not the words, and it is intolerable if anyone shouts at me." Only 30 years old at this time, he was yet to compose his most beautiful   music. By 1802 he was completely deaf and could only imagine how the written notes would sound.

The otosclerosis that deafened Beethoven is now prevented by fluoridated drinking water. Early cases are cured by surgery.

Modern doctors can do more to correct progressive hearing loss than was possible in Beethoven's day. Among seniors the most common causes of progressive deafness is presbyacusis. Appropriately enough, the name means "old man's hearing," but old women have it too. Presbyacusis seems to be related to loud or continuous noise. Excessive noise causes degeneration of the nerves that respond to sound. Some degree of sound nerve degeneration occurs universally in the elderly, just as does gray hair and wrinkles. Nerve deafness cannot be corrected, but it is well to have an examination because other forms of deafness can be improved. As in the case of Beethoven's untreated otosclerosis, when not corrected the hearing organ degenerates and deafness then becomes complete and permanent.

Beethoven the musician was correct in observing that the high notes go first when there is progressive hearing loss. Their absence in the sound spectrum renders speech unintelligible. Individuals with early presbyacusis find that they hear conversation better when there is some background noise. This is probably because, in a noisy environment, speakers unconsciously speak a bit louder and more distinctly. When talking to the hard-of-hearing, this same practice should be followed. Speak more slowly and distinctly. The deaf find that they can understand better if they are able to watch the speaker. It is like reading body language in a foreign country: you don't understand the words but you get the meaning.

• • • •

Tinnitis

Years ago I attended a church whose pride and joy was a beautiful pipe organ. The instrument had been constructed by European craftsmen in the 1800s. Sometimes, unfortunately, the organ would show its age. It would make sounds when it was not supposed to. One or more pipes would squeal even before the keyboard was touched, or continue playing after the organist had stopped. It was like the drone of a bagpipe, barely noticed while the organ was playing, but in the quiet and contemplative moments of worship that old organ could be most distracting. The trouble was in the leather valves which controlled air to each pipe. The leather had shrunk, cracked or crumbled with age, and this allowed air to slip through. The leaking air caused the pipes to squeal without the slightest prompting.

Tinnitus is a hearing abnormality something like that old pipe organ. One has a persistent sensation of sound, but it remains largely unnoticed when there is a noisy environment. At quiet times ear noises become a source of great discomfort. By using a soundproof and echoless sound chamber, it has been found that almost everyone has a little tinnitus. Generally, the sound is a pure tone. It may be like a whistle, a ringing or a buzzing. It may also sound like escaping steam. Tinnitus seldom becomes a problem until after the age of 50.

More than 37 million oldsters have complained about the disease. Tinnitus is associated with advancing deafness. Perhaps it is the sense of an enveloping silence that is so disturbing. Men and women are equally affected by the condition and about half say they hear the sound in only one ear.

Hearing loss resulting from a disturbances in the ear drum or the bony conduction system, produces a low pitched tinnitus. This has the sound of a ventilating fan or of a sea-shell held close to the ear. If there is inflammation present, the sound may be one of a pulsating nature. A similar pulsating noise without any associated hearing loss can also be an early sign of a tumor in or near the region of the ear. This kind of sound can also be made by the partial blockage of an artery with arteriosclerosis.

In other cases, a person can hear strange sounds of his own breathing caused by air turbulence in the throat. These kind of vibrations, which can be detected and heard by a doctor, happen close to the ear and are not true tinnitus. That is to say, they are real and not subjective sounds.

Generally, subjective tinnitus comes from within the nerve portion of the auditory system, of which the exact cause may be impossible to determine. A rushing sound of "white noise" usually accompanies the dizziness of Meniere's disease. (White noise is the sound you get as you turn up the volume of a radio that is not tuned to a station.)

High-pitched whistling or insect sounds are associated with neural high tone deafness. If it starts while you are taking medication, it could be an early sign of drug toxicity. Prolonged use of the drug could have permanent effects. The most common drugs responsible for this high-pitched whistling tinnitis are aspirin, quinine, digitalis and streptomycin.

What can be done about tinnitus? At one time, severing the auditory nerve was tried. This produced total deafness, which was a high price to pay to stop noise in only a small part of the sound spectrum. Cutting only worked half the time and it caused total deafness.

It is important to see a doctor even if little can be done for some tinnitus. A search should be made for a possible cause of the head noise. Often disturbances in the auditory conduction system can be corrected. If this is the case, it will simultaneously relieve deafness and eliminate tinnitus. Discovering and correcting associated cardiovascular disease, tumors and such is well worth the effort and time an examination might take. Even when tinnitus is determined to be caused by degeneration within the neural portion of the auditory system, much still can be done. The use of ambient noise to produce a masking effect has been most helpful. Like that ever-blowing organ pipe, tinnitus is not noticed when there are other sounds to conceal its creaks and squeals.

• • • •

Cataract

At the Kennedy Inauguration ceremony years ago, Robert Frost was in trouble. The 86 year old New England poet had been personally invited to participate by J.F.K. His poem, "The Gift Outright," was to be a focal point of the program. But the independent Mr. Frost had composed, and intended to add, a poetic preface. When he rose to read in the bright sunshine of that crisp January day, the manuscript appeared to be only a glaring piece of white paper. Vice President Johnson got up to shield the sun with his top hat. After a brief struggle, Mr. Frost waved him aside, discarded the useless sheet and recited his older poem.

Robert Frost's poor vision in bright light

was due to cataracts. A cataract is what happens when the clear transparent lens within the eye becomes white and opaque. The medical name for the condition is taken from the similar phenomenon of a river. At the river cataract, clear flowing water breaks into many particles that scatters and reflects light so that it appears white. The more light that is scattered, the greater the white glare.

The lens inside our eye is composed of many transparent cells nourished by surrounding fluid. Growing cells form the lens capsule. As these cells mature they push inward. Unlike old cells on the skin surface they can't rub off. With nowhere to go, cells accumulate within the lens capsule to form an increasingly fibrous, hard-packed mass. The mature cells fragment to die and become opaque.

When vision has so diminished that you can no longer see clearly, the opaque lens should be removed. Operations are done under local anesthesia. But these operations are not without risk because infection can easily set in. There is also the fear of losing eye fluid. Another problem, created when the lens are replaced by a tiny piece of plastic, is the risk of foreign body rejection.

· · · ·

Glaucoma

A scholar born in 1608 with a long-sighted eye ball was in trouble. Eyeglasses had not yet been invented. Driven by his thirst for knowledge, he struggled to force his far-sighted eyes to read books requiring near-sighted vision. His vision become poorer with advancing age. Finally he could read only in very bright light. At age 42, John Milton became completely blind. The last 22 years of his life were the most productive. He was an outstanding classic and Biblical scholar, famous as politician, churchman and literary giant. The event of his blindness is scarcely noticeable amid the continuous outpouring of his genius.

Glaucoma caused John Milton's blindness. Clear structures within the eyeball, (lens, cornea) are kept alive by circulation of a clear fluid. Fluid is secreted at the back of the eye, channeled around the iris and absorbed into the circulation at the front of the eyeball. Bright light causes the iris to contract, producing a pinhole camera effect so that vision improves. But in some people this small pupil also constricted the fluid passageways around the iris, causing pressure to rise within the eyeball. Unfortunately, the weakest spot in the eye is the point where the optic nerve enters to connect retina with brain. Too much pressure punches out the optic nerve, making one forever blind.

Our 20th century has an advantage over Milton's 17th century: eyeball pressure can be easily and quickly measured. If there is a tendency toward glaucoma, medication can be prescribed to relieve that pressure. When needed, an operation will restore the circulatory path. The most com-

mon form of glaucoma among the elderly is associated with a large pupil caused by pressure. Today,
this pressure can be reduced by medication.

So if you would rather read John Milton's
writings than share his blindness, please, go get a
checkup.

8 ADJUSTING TO MATURITY

Night Rising

Dear Aunt Abby,

You are right, most men are cowards when it comes to seeing a doctor. They prefer their infirmity to the possible discomfort that a doctor might cause them. A few men even deny that anything is wrong with them to avoid making the trip to the doctor's office. Somehow, in their mind, to seek aid from someone else becomes a challenge to their personal superiority, wisdom, integrity and independence. By contrast, the weaker sex regularly seeks advice and guidance — and lives longer.

But Uncle Ben is also right in thinking that there are many insignificant reasons for having to get up at night. Older women, as well as men, are aroused from sleep to empty their bladders. Occasional nocturia may be due to drinking liquids late in the day. Delayed diuretic response to tea, coffee or alcohol also keeps the kidneys working on the night shift. Cold or chilling environs have a similar effect.

With age, our kidneys do not work as efficiently as when we were younger. The kidneys must, in a sense, work overtime to get their job done. Check the ankles at day's end for swelling. Push firmly with the thumb against the ankle bone. If your thumb leaves an impression, there is excess fluid in the tissues. This is called edema. Edema may be caused by prolonged standing, sitting and varicose veins, as well as poor circulation. Water is held in the ankle tissues by gravity. Lying down and getting the feet up will cancel the effect of gravity so that the water goes back into circulation. This has the same result as getting a drink of water. The kidneys secrete more urine, thus, rousing one from sleep in the middle of the night.

I suspect Uncle Ben's nocturia, however, may not have such an insignificant cause. Four out of five older men have benign prostatic hypertrophy (BPH) and this possibility should be investigated. The prostate gland forms a ring about the urinary bladder outlet. When the prostate grows larger (hypertrophy), emptying the bladder becomes more difficult. The size and force of the urinary stream is diminished and emptying takes longer. Responding to the obstruction, muscles of the bladder will hypertrophy. In spite of the stronger muscular action, the bladder does not completely empty. The urine remaining in the bladder after urinating reduces the additional amount of urine the bladder can accept before it reaches capacity. Frequent bathroom visits, dribbling, and urgency become bothersome overflow symptoms of BPH. The stagnant pool of urine remaining in the bladder after voiding also invites infection. Infection can additionally cause frequency, fever and burning on urination.

Less noticeable but of more serious consequence to urinary tract obstruction is the greater pressure the blockage creates. This pressure distends the passage, which also affects the kidney and impairs renal function. The blood pressure then rises to furnish the higher secretory pressure the kidneys must now require. Uremia and stroke may eventually be the likely consequences of putting off a visit to the doctor.

Modern anesthesia can safely minimize the pain and discomfort of surgery. Operating techniques with pencil-size instruments can remove the prostatic obstruction without even having to cut the skin. Uncle Ben should screw up his courage and go see a doctor. The consequences from supposing wrongly, that getting up several times a night is normal for older men, are too serious. At least, after a check-up, both of you will sleep better.

Your loving nephew,

. . . .

BPH

"Life begins at forty" for benign prostatic hypertrophy (BPH).

At that age the prostate resumes growth in four out of every five men. Prostates then continue to grow for another 40 years.

The term "benign" suggests that the prostate's gradual enlargement is kind and gentle rather than malignant. Indeed, only about one in three benign prostates ever cause significant trouble. BPH generally takes twenty years of growing to produce symptoms. When, at about the time of retirement, a man notices that his urinary stream has diminished and he begins to get up during the night, BPH is announcing its presence.

While the growth of BPH may be slow and gradual, the symptoms are sometimes sudden and severe. Hypertrophied tissue in the prostate can become acutely congested and swollen, causing sudden urinary shut-off. Acute urinary retention is an emergency often brought on by chilling or a delay in voiding. It may also follow use of alcohol or medicines such as tranquilizers and cold decongestants.

The prostate is a plum-size structure which surrounds the outlet of the bladder. Its function is to add fluid to the germ cells in semen. The part of the prostate where BPH occurs is in the center and adjacent to the urinary passage. (Surprisingly, cancer of the prostate does not usually start here, but will grow to produce obstruction and many of the same symptoms as BPH. Although cancer is sometimes found during the operation for BPH, the two conditions are not related.)

BPH symptoms result when enlargement obstructs the outflow of urine. The ability to completely empty the bladder becomes impossible. Urine remaining in the bladder becomes easily infected and it is stubborn to clear. Moreover, difficulty in voiding creates increased pressure which spreads like a chain-reaction to the kidneys, the circulatory system and the heart. Distention of the kidneys impairs kidney function and can eventually lead to uremia. In the centuries before modern surgery, uremia, stroke or heart attack was often the fatal ending of this "kind" and "gentle" disease.

Surgical removal of the overgrown tissue is the most satisfactory treatment for benign prostatic hypertrophy. The operation is very safe and is usually done without cutting the skin. Only the overgrown tissue is removed. The remaining prostate continues to secrete fluid after surgery. But there is one difference: semen is now discharged into the bladder, rather than to the outside.

. . . .

Impotence

> "Then Abraham laughed and said to himself, 'can a son be born to a man who is 100 years old? ' "
> — Gen. 17:17.

As a young physician I learned about the sex life of seniors from my patients. There was the

84- year-old retired copper miner who came to me with a venereal disease. The law required doctors to report VD and the circumstances of its acquisition. That is how I learned my patient's story. A widower, he was living alone in a small house next to a dry cleaning establishment. One afternoon a woman came to his door. She told him that she was .50 cents short of having enough money to pay her cleaning bill. Would he, she asked, give her a half dollar in exchange for sex? The old man was ready, willing and able. And the price was right — even for a retiree on limited income.

Then there was Sergeant R, the last of the U. S. Army Indian scouts. He was a boy when friendly Apaches helped the army track down and capture Geronimo. That was back in 1886. Before World War II he was a colorful part of every Fourth of July parade. It was during that war that I delivered a child to his 24-year-old wife.

The old Indian told me that his people took care of their old men by giving them a young wife. It was a practical kind of social security, much like that the Israelites provided King David. The newlyweds would leave the tribe to go off on their "honeymoon." They did not return unless the wife became pregnant. The elderly groom, having proved himself, was again accepted into the tribal council. It was the custom for the medicine-man to give the groom a concoction which was supposed to be an aphrodisiac. It was also the custom, and a matter of some pride as well, that the medicine was brought back unused. The medicinal effect of an aphrodisiac is by its psychological impact. The virtue of this Indian remedy was that it worked without being ingested, so there were no side effects or addictions.

Impotence is a concern to men of all ages and from every society. In overpopulated Asia, the rhinoceros is almost extinct because its horn is reputed to have magical properties. Doctors, as well as Indian Medicine Men, know that impotence results as much from worry and mind-set as from the failure of hormones.

There is an additional modifying factor in the elderly. While seniors continue to find interest and a pleasant satisfaction in the mental aspects of sex, they no longer possess the physical strength to indulge themselves. Intercourse takes more energy than it does to climb two flights of stairs. In most other sports, one ceases to be a participant at half the age of us seniors.

Oh! —about that Indian baby. It was a boy. He was the first of the old scout's children to be born in a hospital. Naturally the son was named Big Shot R——. Only a "big shot" would get as much attention as that Indian baby received in the hospital.

•   •   •   •

Sleep

"[I]nnocent sleep, sleep that knits up
the ravelled sleeve of care."
　　　　　　　　— Shakespeare

We have all experienced MacBeth's difficulty of falling asleep when our minds are stimulated or troubled. Often the mind will work as we sleep to solve our problem.

Brain wave studies by electroencephalogram show that sleep is a very complex state. During light sleep, where there are rapid eye movements (REM sleep), brain wave recordings reveal the brain busily rearranging and storing information. Infants and children have a great deal of REM sleep and it is attributed to their developing nervous systems.

Although most of the dreams we recall occur during light sleep, nightmares and sleep walking come in deep sleep. Light and deep sleep alternate to form a pattern most easily seen in infants. With maturity we learn to adapt to the cycle of night and day. For most of us, night is reserved for sleep. And generally, we consolidate our sleep into a single episode averaging seven and one-half hours. The electroencephalogram, however, detects the infantile cycle of increased and decreased brain activity throughout the entire 24 hour day.

Sleep studies on oldsters show that they have much less REM sleep. This is attributed to our diminished, and less acute, senses. We also have fewer challenging and stimulating problems to keep us awake. The sleep cycle of childhood reappears in the elderly, but with a difference. We have much less deep sleep. Instead of going from light to deep sleep and back to light sleep, the pattern is from awake to light sleep to awake. Studies also show that our sleep time is increased, but our personal judgement of the amount of sleep we get is fallacious: we get more sleep than we think we do.

By nature we are adapted to alternating cycles of light and dark. Dull winter skies and bright indoor lighting provides little contrast between day and night. Experiments have shown that people sleep more soundly if exposed to bright light during day time hours. So get outside for a little sunshine whenever possible.

Many conditions coincidental to aging may interfere with light sleep. Heart or lung disease may make it difficult to lie down. Kidney and bladder function are often disturbing at night. Caffeine and stimulating medications taken late in the day can leave us staring into blackness. Pains and discomforts, easily minimized during the day when we are active, become intolerable with nightfall.

What to do? What to do? First of all, either avoid or treat sleep-disturbing factors before you reach for a sleeping pill. Sleeping pills eliminate REM sleep. Moreover, the drugged condition does not provide the restorative rest we all need. Fatigue from physical activity is the natural and best sedative. Muscle relaxation in bed can be enhanced by consciously tensing, stretching and then relaxing muscle groups in turn. Start with the feet and legs, working up to the hands and arms. End with the neck and face. Finally take some deep breaths and let everything relax, imagining your heavy limbs are supported by a cloud.

Sleep drugs have had a long and checkered history. Alcohol and opium date from antiquity. In this century, bromides and barbiturates had their "day." And then there was Thalidomide producing mutations in the unborn. Now we hear of Halcyon causing confusion, amnesia and anxiety in President Bush. So, if you must take something, never take it regularly. My personal preference is one of the antihistamines given for allergy or medication for motion sickness. These produce drowsiness as a side effect when first used. They, like all the others, are less effective when taken regularly.

• • • •

Fever

Fever has long been accepted as a symptom of illness. It is usually accompanied by headache, muscle ache and a general lassitude. There may also be various associated discomforts, such as sore throat, stomach ache, cough etc. When present, local symptoms, such as an infection, are assumed to be the cause of the fever. Be warned, however, that a temperature rise can be caused by outside environmental manipulation, in which case there will be no local symptoms. General discomforts, like headaches, muscle aches, tiredness, etc., often have other causes. But the general rule is that whenever there are local symptoms accompanied by a fever, your illness is probably due to infection.

Fever is defined as a temperature above the body's normal reading. Normal temperature is accepted as 98.6 Fahrenheit when taken under the tongue. Temperature taken rectally is a degree higher and skin temperature a degree lower, all of which suggests that normal has some variations. Actually, normal is even less precise. It was established by averaging the norm of many "normal" people whose physical make up was as varied as their body forms and occupations.

While healthy people all stick close to normal temperature, each has a daily variation of one or more degrees. Temperature is always subnormal before awakening. This is so regular that women can accurately pinpoint ovulation on the exact morning of a temperature change. Activity causes temperature to rise. Vigorous activity will temporarily push it into the fever zone. Fever, or rather higher temperature, is induced whenever environmental conditions prevent the body from getting rid of its excess heat.

Fever acts as kind of a guide to the seriousness of the infection. Babies and children respond with high temperatures to minor infections. One or two degrees isn't serious because it can be produced by activity or environment. When an adult gets a fever equivalent to a child's, he is really sick.

Fever is usually more serious with the elderly for the following reason. Healthy seniors have lower metabolisms, which means that the fluctuations in their their daily temperature may seldom reach the "normal" 98.6 F. So when they do get a temperature above 100 F it could mean that, relatively, it is three or four degrees above a senior's daily norm, not "just a little above normal."

I recall a 70-year-old woman who had symptoms of appendicitis but a fever of only 99 F. The blood count also was low. We were busy so she was put to bed for observation. Our recheck at day's end showed little change, but fortunately we operated anyway. The appendix had already ruptured. She might have died had we not had antibiotics.

Many elderly have lost their resistance to infections. White cells and the restorative forces don't properly mobilize to produce fever. So fever is not a reliable indicator of the seriousness of the illness. Oldsters are different from "normal" people.

•   •   •   •

Melancholy

Little drops of water, tiny grains of sand.
Make the mighty ocean and the solid land.

In every life "a little rain must fall," but sometimes it appears to be a deluge. We have all had our share of failures and losses. Our black mood of disappointment is usually only temporary. Life goes on. New vistas of opportunity open. Eventually, we put the matter behind us. We look ahead and "cheer up."

Unfortunately, negative incidents of life can be especially traumatic for the elderly. The aged are short of time and have diminishing abilities. The opportunity for a "come back" is always there but can we do any better with a second try this late in life? The gloomy state of the elderly is compounded by the number and seriousness of troubles and future uncertainties.

Clinically significant depression reaches a peak in the population after age 60. It affects more than 2 percent of men and 4 percent of women beyond that age. Depression is believed to be a reaction to cumulative stress from individual circumstances. For many, retirement is quickly followed by changes in living conditions, financial worries, degenerating physical abilities, and the partings of life-long companions. When living longer, one suffers loneliness by the loss of loved ones who do not live as long. So the mournful mood is seen to grow out of the unhappiness and misery of one's everyday experiences.

Melancholy (the word means black bile), with lowering mood, is a normal experience following the loss of something important or the failure to obtain something hoped for. It is felt by persons at all ages as illustrated by the "tired housewife syndrome." An old saying reminds us that we need to have our "bad" days to appreciate our "good" ones. Part of our inbuilt emotional mechanism places blame for our gloomy condition upon ourselves. We become preoccupied with our mistakes and failings. We think , "If only I had done thus and so. . . . If only I were well. . . . or young enough . . . ." The introspection runs over and over. Subconsciously we convince ourselves that we have brought misfortune upon ourselves. We feel guilty, inadequate, worthless. Melancholy is our punishment.

All illnesses produce some degree of melancholy. In fact, unhappiness is almost synonymous with ill health. But the black thoughts of unconscious hostility toward self can overwhelm and degenerate into serious illness. Preoccupation with looking at the bleak side leads to loss of interest in life's possibilities. Forgotten are the satisfactions and pleasures of other experiences. To make matters worse there is difficulty in concentration and loss of memory. Decisions are postponed, sleep is disturbed and one has little energy for tasks at hand. This morbid, pessimistic and hopeless attitude can degenerate into neurotic or psychotic illness.

Now, if you are finding it too difficult to "cheer up," get some help. Research has shown that our mood changes are caused by the release of neurotransmitters within the brain. Neurotransmitters are needed to permit nerves to communicate with each other. Psychiatric consultation can be restorative in many circumstances by altering the way one thinks about self. Additionally, modern pharmacology has developed medications which will block certain overabundant neurotransmitters. Other medication can replace neurotransmitters that are in short supply. Normalcy depends upon the proper balance of at least four neurotransmitters. So take the chance, share your melancholy with a psychologist. You will be happier with the result.

• • • •

Happiness

What is the secret of happiness? My patient should have been enjoying her "years of contentment." Instead, she came to me for treatment of minor complaints which had little physical basis. Subconsciously she was using illness as a means to gain attention. She was unaware that there is a difference between the affection she craved and the sympathy she was getting.

Her face was lined and tense as she was saying, "I keep getting these pains in my stomach . . . and lots of gas . . . and then my head aches . . . and my glasses aren't right, so I can't read . . . and my heart hurts and beats hard. I go to bed but I can't sleep. In the morning, I just want to stay in bed. I don't feel like going out . . . I'm so tired all the time."

I too, was getting tired — tired of her "organ recital" and litany of complaints. I appreciate why psychologists favor a couch for their patients and then sit outside the patient's view. That way they remain detached while listening to the patient "ventilate."

I had to face the music, so I broke into her monologue.

"How was it a month ago, at Christmas time?," I asked.

She thought a moment, her face relaxing.

"I was felling better then," she said.

I saw an opening to a new subject.

"Did you get some nice presents?"

"No, not really".

"Anything unusual happen?"

She smiled while recalling the memory of her grandson giving her a piece of ceramic he had made at school. It seems he had botched the paint job and ended up making it all black.

"What did you do when you opened his ugly present?," I asked.

"Oh," she said, "I pretended I was real

pleased and I told him I liked it a lot."

"Why did you do that?" I probed.

"Because," she said, "it would have hurt him if I hadn't liked it, and I like to make children happy — especially at Christmas."

I remarked, "I think you have just told me the secret for happiness. When we give or do something to please another, the happiness we leave returns to the giver. The recipient of the gift discovers happiness through the appreciation of the gift. The Lord loveth a cheerful giver," but the appreciative recipient is doubly blessed.

Seniors who are no longer able to give to others can still show appreciation for what others do for them. Keep happy.

• • • •

Mental and Physical Health

"To escape the turmoils of the world, we should cultivate our gardens."
— Voltaire

Voltaire was a free thinker. His outspoken opinions kept him continually at odds with his more complacent and frequently hostile contemporaries. At age 21 he spent a year in the Bastille. For 28 of his remaining years he lived outside his native France in flight or in exile. He died shortly after returning to Paris at age 84, while producing a play.

Voltaire's skepticism of religion led to his belief that happiness could only be found by returning to nature. Most of us will agree that the quiet beauty of a garden does much to restore peace to the soul. But is the body also restored by working in the garden? Modern research seems to verify Voltaire's conclusions.

Animals and humans are endowed with an arousal mechanism that releases hormones to better enable them to meet or escape physical dangers. Civilization has diminished many dangers for which animal alertness and muscular response were appropriate defenses. Instead, Americans today face an intellectually challenging environment. Our aggressiveness, rivalries, and striving to achieve bring rewards in our social and business worlds. Anger, hostility, impatience and worry trigger physical arousal, which in turn creates stress.

If the arousal mechanism is activated often and not discharged, our defensive body chemistry leads to illness. High blood pressure, heart attack, headache, and an upset stomach may result from stress. Research indicates that the consequences of serious disease does not occur when there is a physical response to stress. As we "cultivate our gardens," we can discharge our harmful emotions.

It is the sympathetic nervous system that automatically responds to danger and stress by altering body chemistry. Until recently, doctors believed that the system was beyond voluntary control. Now we know that a biological "feedback" network exists. Our thought processes can relieve stress. Good thoughts produce altered body chemistry that is healing. Learning a different behavioral response to stress is effective and healthy. Wouldn't it be a wonderful accomplishment to give up all those pills?

The way to modify body response to stress is through meditation and relaxation. The healing techniques of each are practiced in Eastern religions, but have not been taken seriously in the West. Briefly, the components are: a comfortable position; repetition of a prayer, phrase, or sound; the adoption of a passive attitude toward intruding thoughts; and a quiet environment. So we return to Voltaire's quiet garden to escape from the turmoils (and diseases) of the world. Now is the time to begin. Plant carrots for a border.

. . . .

Mileau Therapy

> *"He taught laughin' and grief"*
> — Alice in Wonderland.

Does the above quote make you smile? It is believed that the author, Charles Dodgson (Lewis Carroll) wrote this apparent nonsense in rebellion against his occupation. How imprecise for a mathematician to use words that only sound like "Latin" and "Greek." And how illogical for a logician to lump together the extremes of human emotion. Children enjoy his stories with flights of imagination and absurd improbabilities. But it requires an adult mind to fully appreciate hidden truths in illogical thoughts.

How odd to link laughter with grief. In our society we seek to avoid grief. We hide the unlovely, the handicapped and those who must suffer in our institutions. We reason the institutions are better equipped to give them care. We soon forget the maladies and misfortunes of others when they are out of sight. When we have thus comfortably taken grief out of our lives, we can then laugh.

Scientists have described laughter as "a spontaneous natural reflex involving 15 facial muscles, associated with certain irreplaceable noises and alteration in breathing." The only utilitarian value to laughing appears to be to relieve tension. The laugh reflex occurs when there is a sudden release of tension brought on by danger or discomfort, either apparent or real. To tickle someone, for example, is actually a physical assault upon that person. Laughter ensues when it is perceived that no harm is intended by the attacker. Is laughter only the luxury of a primordial reflex, or does it possess healthy and restorative value?

The paradox of laughter and grief was brought to my attention by an article in a Tacoma newspaper. The front page story was an interview with an elderly couple visiting the Tacoma area. In the interview, the couple talked about their personal experiences working with Albert Schweitzer in his jungle hospital in Africa.

In my experience, hospitals are asylums of quietude where patients endure pain—and sometimes die. Loved ones suffer quietly in anguish and grief. The 350 patients of Schweitzer's antiquated institution were served by an inadequate volunteer staff and barely supported by charitable donations. Facilities were crowded by the continued press of the diseased, distressed, and disabled. Food and medicine were never adequate.

In addition, there was the sorrowful misfortune of having to care for a leper colony of 150 with inadequate medical supplies and equipment With conditions as they were, the lepers had little hope, especially of a cure. Surely Lambarene was a place of sorrow and grief. Yet, our Tacoma visitors reported that Lambarene was a place where you could always hear laughter.

Americans have come to believe that modern medicine can work wonders. Yet there are many situations where wonders do not exist. As Samuel Johnson put it in the year of his death, "My diseases are an asthma and a dropsy and what is less curable, seventy-five." What can be done about diseases that seem to have no remedy?

Recent advances in brain and behavorial sciences have revealed that personal interactions have a marked influence upon our physiologic response to illness. Providing the proper social and physical environment can mobilize the brain's own healing potential. Applying this concept is called "Milieu Therapy." It engenders better health through environment, hope and encouragement.

Our health care facilities have become sterile and impersonal institutions that have succumbed to demands of managerial efficiency. In assuming all responsibility for their client's daily care, hospitals have stifled that internal life-affirming force that enables patients to cope with incurable illnesses. But some long-term care facilities are waking up to the problem. They are beginning to use milieu therapy to restore self-esteem and to impart to the individual a sense of personal control over his or her life.

Wouldn't it be great to hear a little laughter amid all that grief?

• • • •

Touch

"Who touched me?"
—Luke 8:45

Doctor Luke, and most physicians before our generation, accepted the fact that healing could be accomplished by touching. More than magic, touch is communication. With touch, sensory messages are given and received almost simultaneously. Eyes and ears may witness events just as a TV camera does. But to experience life, one must reach out and touch it. Modern healers are again recognizing that this most personal of all our senses can be an important therapeutic tool.

Children seek to escape the warm, soft, protective contact of the mother's arms. They strive for individuality with their very own private living space. Maturity is achieved when they learn to mimic the customary pattern of adult behavior.

In the Orient, a person's self is reinforced by pressing the hands together and keeping the arms close to the sides. The submissive attitude of bowing the head even breaks eye contact. The self is thus effectively isolated from the other. The isolation of individuals can result either from voluntary withdrawal or by helpless rejection. Those isolated from society become outcasts—untouchables.

In the West we do not have a caste system, but we do have old people who are seldom touched. Our habit is to shake hands. The custom came to us from the age of chivalry. Emancipated serfs adopted the behavior pattern of freemen. Unfortunately, the only free men they knew were their former masters and these autocratic noblemen had reason to be suspicious of others. Grasping the outstretched hand of another not only served to keep the other at arm's length, but it assured that the hand held no weapon.

Within the Latin and Islamic cultures, friends

are welcomed with an embrace. In childhood, hugging is natural when personal space is shared with mother. As adults, this intimate behavior re-affirms the unity of mankind. It reinforces our natural need to feel trust, acceptance and security. And in community we have life.

In retirement, our failing senses and the infirmaties of age gradually separate us from life's mainstream. When ill we are placed in the care of strangers in unfamiliar surroundings. Unfeeling machines, probes and piercing instruments penetrate our personal space. Once hospitalized, we lose control over our body and any say about its destiny. Our innermost secrets are yanked from us to be translated into incomprehensible words and numbers.

Intellectually, we accept such methods of science as helpful to our doctor. But in our subconscious, we find it difficult to relate hostile acts with friendly assistance. Modern medicine has become mechanized and impersonal. The gentle touch of a doctor's hand, used in bygone days, is no longer required to gather information. But touch is still needed to convey an unspoken message of care, concern and understanding. The ill and elderly must be touched to validate that they are part of community — and not untouchables. The impersonal sponge bath and back rub may save the skin, but it does not restore the soul. We cling to life by holding hands. Have you touched someone today?

• • • •

Skin

It is a rare senior who still possesses a perfect skin. I do not refer to the wrinkles and sags which come because the skin thins and loses elasticity. These are the normal physiologic changes due to age. The worrisome imperfections are those blotches and bumps that begin to appear on a previously smooth and unblemished surface.

Recently, a large clinic carefully checked all patients more than 64-years-old. Almost 90 percent had more than 10 unattractive wart-like spots diagnosed as seborrheic keratosis. These are nonmalignant tumors. Seborrheic keratoses grow from pin-point size to more than an inch in diameter. Usually they are a quarter inch across, flat and slightly raised. To the touch, they feel somewhat greasy and wart-like. They also seem stuck on the skin because they are not attached at the edges. Where exposed on the face and neck, they may become quite dark. Seborrheic keratosis can be confused with other skin tumors, but aside from unsightliness, they do no harm. Applications of castor oil or olive oil will soften the surface so that the thickness can be gently rubbed off. This will temporarily improve appearance. If you don't want it to come back, have a doctor destroy the base.

Other forms of keratosis bear watching. Senile keratosis is a different and more serious skin imperfection. As the name implies, it does strike the elderly. However, the actual occurrence of senile keratosis correlates better with old skin rather than old age. Skin becomes prematurely aged by overexposure to the sun. Just compare the back of your hand to the skin on your abdomen. Persons with fair complexions are particularly susceptible. Except among avid sun-bathers, and possibly belly dancers, the condition is confined to the face, neck and back of the hands.

Some authorities believe senile keratosis begins as a freckle. The patch enlarges, becoming dry and scaly. The scales fall off or are picked away so that usual thickness is not above the surrounding skin. There is a thickening beneath the surface, however, which gives a stiffness to the area. Keratosis is a pre-malignant condition.

When one avoids exposure to the sun's rays, senile keratosis may remain inactive for many years. Dryness of the skin's surface can be remedied by the application of a bland oil or grease. Any changes, such as thickening, breakdown of the surface, or accelerated growth should be checked by your doctor immediately. This sudden growth could signal the beginning of a skin cancer. At this early stage, cancer can be easily and effectively treated.

Active seniors orient their retirement, recreation and travel plans to the great outdoors in the season of sunshine. Hats, gloves and sunscreen preparations can keep your skin more youthful. Protection from ultraviolet radiation can reduce your chances of having senile keratosis.

· · · ·

Teeth

> *"Grandmother, what big teeth you have!"*
> — Little Red Riding Hood.

It's no fairy tale for some grandmothers (and grandfathers too) when it is discovered that their teeth appear to be growing longer. The teeth actually aren't getting longer. Rather, it is a person's receding gums that leave more of the tooth exposed. "Bigger" teeth are the result of gum disease. And it is a serious problem. The exposed root, unprotected by gum, is more likely to develop cavities. Teeth become loose and eventually fall out because bone around the roots is reabsorbed. The fancy name for gum disease is periodontia. It only means, "around the teeth." At some time in life 95 percent of Americans have periodontia. When nothing is done about it, these people can someday expect to look like the wolf.

Periodontal disease is generally the result of inadequate dental care. A film constantly forms on our teeth, just as it does in the toilet bowl. Dental film is called plaque. It is composed of mucous and bacteria. When plaque is left undisturbed for as little as a week or ten days it may became calcified.

It is then called calculus or scale.

Calculus irritates the gum tissue and wedges it away from the tooth. The gum becomes red, sore, puffy and bleeds easily. Pockets form in the gum. They trap particles of food and soon infection sets in. At this point breath odor is enough to curdle a granddaughters kiss — even one as nice as Little Red Riding Hood.

American promotional genius offers some easy solutions to the problem. Ads tell us to buy mouth wash to help our breaths smell better. Mouth washes use scents to mask odors. The active ingredients, commonly alcohol or boric acid, have only a slight temporary effect on bacteria. In periodontia they are about as effective as salt water. Gadgeteers ballyhoo the water jet for cleaning teeth. But a water jet won't remove plaque any better than a stream of water cleans the kitchen sink. When periodontitis is present, the force irritates the tender gums.

There is no way to clean teeth more effectively than to scrub them with a toothbrush and get in between them with dental floss. A brush will do a better job when used with toothpaste. Opaque toothpaste, however, contains an abrasive grit. Newer pastes contain ingredients which soften and remove plaque

Abrasive grit in food once wore dental surfaces flat by age 60. At 70, the teeth were worn to the gums. But seniors can chew better today without running the risk of wearing out their teeth.

Natural tooth cleaners are the crunchy foods like hardtack and raw vegetables.

Smoking increases plaque, because it stimulates the production of mucous. In addition to being an irritant, smoke is a carcinogen and depletes vitamin C, which is essential for healthy gums. The first sign of scurvy is often sore bleeding gums. Alcohol in concentrations stronger than a mouthwash will also irritate tender mouth tissues. Just killing bacteria on the surface does not cure deep-seated diseases.

. . . .

Toenails

Some seniors go to a podiatrist about as frequently as others go to a beauty salon or barber shop. It isn't to make their feet more lovely, just more comfortable. The usual problems are painful corns, callosities and bunions. Many go just to have their toenails cut. Old toenails can get tougher than an old curmudgeon. Dinky finger nail scissors won't cut them. Besides, with advancing age it becomes more difficult to reach or to even see them.

As the nails grow out from the root, additional material is added from the nail bed. It dries out and hardens to become tough as the hoof of a horse, which is the horse's toenail. Sometimes thickening and distortion of toenails result from injury. Most distortion comes from the constant pressure of tight shoes and stockings. Fungus infection will also distort nails.

Toenail trimming is not covered by Medicare, so you may have to do it yourself, or have it done by a good friend. Toenails are easier to cut after they are softened by soaking the feet in warm water. Plus, you may need heavier nail cutters. Ordinary scissors are too broad and don't provide enough leverage. Always cut toenails straight across. Rounding corners may lead to an ingrown nail, because weight bearing pushes flesh up in front of the growing nail corners. If this happens, protect the skin with a wisp of cotton pushed between the nail and the flesh of the toe with a flat toothpick. It is also a good idea to smooth off the freshly cut nail with an emery board or file. It is possible to file tough nails instead of cutting them. This can be a slow process, though, unless you use a metal file from your tool box.

9

EPILOGUE

Secret Fountain of Youth

Research into cell chromosomes and deoxyribonucleic acid (DNA) demonstrate that cell division and replication is determined by genes located in the cell. Individuals start life as a fertilized germ-cell which divides to form two, then four, etc. Division continues to produce the millions of cells that make up the human body. At each division, chromosomes in each cell must split, then replicate themselves for each "daughter" cell to pass along the genetic information.

Even more remarkable is cell specialization. Bone, muscle, skin, and brain cells are vastly different and serve different functions. Yet, they all descended and were modified from that original germ-cell. It is believed that the DNA program within a cell not only determines the kind of cell it will become, but when it will function and for how long. Thus, fetal organs serve their purpose then become non-functional in later life. In like manner, genes turn on cells years after theirdormant fetal period. While a baby will double its weight in a few months, all tissues and organs finally stop growing.   Life is a matter of change: of conception, growth, maturity and senescence, in orderly fashion.

Man lives 50 times as long as a mouse. He has 10 thousand times as many cells. Any one of these cells can become transformed to cancer. Yet, the two species have about the same number of tumors over a lifetime. Human cells grown in culture will outlive mice cell cultures. Cell culture taken from a baby will outlive that taken from an adult. So it appears that age must be programmed within the cell itself— in the DNA of chromosomes.

At the time a cell divides, chromosomes split and replicate in each daughter cell. Radiation or toxic chemicals can interfere at cell division by breaking the chain and altering the genetic code. Genetic change may result in cell mutation and cancer. It is believed higher forms of life live longer because they have a better mechanism to repair damaged chromosomes. Fortunately, most cells reproduce, serve their function and die. Repair lies in properly restoring and duplicating the genes whenever the cell dividesAdult cells have had more divisions and will have sustained greater damage than juvenile cells. Cancer is therefore more common in the elderly since cancer arises from losing cell specialization information. A mutated cell eventually may only replicate itself, reverting to an embryonic growth pattern. Growth, with no other function, kills the host.

Part of the "repair" process lies in prompt removal of mutated cells—cells which are only damaged a little but don't function exactly right. Removal is accomplished by our immune system. The immune system is able to distinguish foreign material, like bacteria or transplants, from our own body cells. With AIDS (Acquired Immune Deficiency Syndrome) a virus penetrates the body's own cells and knocks out the immune system. Then there is little to combat disease, so illness progresses rapidly.

Tissue and organ transplants are possible only when a proper cross-match is made. A transplant is accepted because it looks like "self." Transplanted cells must not challenge the immune system if the transplant is to take. A mutant cell should challenge since it must be removed even though the cell was originally part of the body. With age, even without AIDS, our immune systems deteriorate and we become less resistant to disease. It is of interest that in Alzheimer's disease, diabetes, and atherosclerosis, large masses of mutated cells are found. Senescence is probably the accumulation of too much dysfunctional tissue composed of mutated cells.

Deterioration of immune systems with age is confirmed by a 1992, 50-year study of 35 thousand workers at Hanford Nuclear Reservation showing risks from small doses of radiation. The study found that, for all adults up to age 58, the risk of cancer doubled with exposure to 26 rems of radiation. After that age the risk doubled after only 5 rems of exposure. Beyond age 62, doubling occurred with less than 1 rem. Radiation causes cell mutation in all persons exposed, regardless of age. But younger workers have a stronger immune system which recognizes mutant cells and stops them before they develop into cancer.

A distinguishing feature of all long-lived species is their lower metabolism. This is the rate at which they generate heat and energy from their food. Birds and mice have high metabolisms and live few years. Man and elephants live longer at a more leisurely pace. Metabolism is basically oxidation, "burning up" food. It combines food elements (carbon, hydrogen and nitrogen) with atmospheric oxygen to extract energy and leave a residue of carbon dioxide, water and urea. As this metabolic process is done in stages, a number of intermediate substances are produced which are toxic to living cells in which metabolism takes place. These toxins are able to break and interfere with chromosome gene network integrity. This can produce cell mutation just as radiation and toxic chemicals do. One might truthfully say that eating is killing us. Usually people who are underweight and who have low metabolisms live longer than those who don't. Reduced coloric intake lessens the possibility of oxidation damage to the DNA resulting in fewer tumors and longer life.

As noted above, higher life forms have a superior repair process. The many chromosome breaks that could lead to cell mutation are harmless when repaired quickly. Gene repair is enhanced by a number of substances identified as "anti-oxidants." Anti-oxidants tie up toxic intermediate metabolic substances which could disrupt DNA chromosome chains. The principle anti-oxidants have been identified and are readily available. They are vitamin C, vitamin E, beta carotene, selenium, glutathione and methionine.

High uric acid blood level also is an anti-oxidant and seems to work in the same manner as vitamin C. Gout is a disease caused by abnormally high uric acid levels. Gout was first noted among upper class aristocracy who consumed too much rich food. Could protection of their DNA genetic code by uric acid be the reason gouty persons are often rich, successful and brainy?

Hormones play an important role in life, notably at puberty and menopause. Normally they enhance cell reproduction, but they have also been linked to many cancers. The price of longevity and sex is an increase in cell mutations and cancer. A different hormone, dehydroepiandrosterone (DHEA), has been identified as a hormone that appears to prevent cancer and mutations. Blood level of DHEA increases to its highest point at ages 25 to 30. Then it gradually decreases. By age 70, DHEA is only 5 percent to 10 percent of its peak value. Experimental use of DHEA has prevented cancer and extended longevity. DHEA incidentally prevented obesity. So here is another chicken versus egg situation. Food restriction alone will result in fewer cancers and longer life.

Aging is a fundamental life process, like infancy and puberty. Life extension, presently, seems to be only a prolongation of senescence. More desirable are additional years with all the abilities preserved as we have in middle life. Can DHEA turn back the clock? There is no fountain of youth: it is all DNA programmed within the cell. We can't alter our DNA genes, but we can protect them from greater injury by the way we live. We can also make longer-life more meaningful by continuing to use the abilities we have developed in becoming the "chronologically advantaged."

APPENDIX

Model of Living Will:

DIRECTIVE TO PHYSICIANS

Directive made this _____ day of _____, 1993.

I, _____, being of sound mind, willfully, and voluntarily make known my desire that my life shall not be artificially prolonged under the circumstances set forth below, and do hereby declare that:

(a) If at any time I should have an incurable injury, disease, or illness certified to be a terminal condition by two physicians, and where the application of life-sustaining procedures would serve only to artificially prolong the moment of my death and where my physician determines that my death is imminent whether or not life-sustaining procedures are utilized, I direct that such procedures be withheld or withdrawn, and that I be permitted to die naturally.

(b) In the absence of my ability to give directions regrading the use of such life-sustaining procedures, it is my intention that this directive shall be honored by my family and physician(s) as the final expression of my legal right to refuse medical or surgical treatment and I accept the consequences from such refusal.

(c) I understand the full import of this directive and I am emotionally and mentally competent to make this directive.

_____

The Declarer has been personally known to me and I believe her to be of sound mind.

_____
witness

_____
witness